Thomas James Owen. *William Watts Folwell Collection, Minnesota Historical Society.*

"Dear Friends at Home..."

The Letters and Diary of Thomas James Owen, Fiftieth New York Volunteer Engineer Regiment, during the Civil War

Edited
and with an Introduction
by
Dale E. Floyd

Historical Division
Office of Administrative Services
Office of the Chief of Engineers

For sale by the Superintendent of Documents, U.S. Government Printing Office
Washington, D.C. 20402

FOREWORD

This is the fourth publication in the series of Corps of Engineers Historical Studies. The first three contained the official reports of Army Engineers. This one is a little different. It reproduces the personal letters and diary of an Engineer soldier who served in the Civil War.

Union forces in the Civil War needed far more Engineers than the Regular Army could furnish. Volunteer Engineers, who entered the Army for wartime service only, supported operations just as did the regulars. Their contributions ranged from constructing ponton bridges under fire to building field fortifications for siege operations.

Thomas Owen's letters and diary reveal the life and duties of a volunteer Engineer who served as a sergeant and company-grade officer. These writings convey his reactions to the extreme conditions of wartime, from the rigors of combat to the boredom of camp life. For their insights into the thoughts and feelings of an Engineer at war and descriptions of Civil War combat engineering, they should still interest those of us who serve as Army Engineers.

Paul Taylor
Colonel, Corps of Engineers
Chief of Staff

TABLE OF CONTENTS

Editor's Preface vii

Introduction xi

Thomas Owen's Letters, 8 April 1862–2 May 1865 1

Thomas Owen's Diary, 29 April–18 May 1864 111

Index to Letters 119

EDITOR'S PREFACE

Thomas James Owen's letters and diary came to the Historical Division, U.S. Army Corps of Engineers, through the efforts of several people. Paul Trap, a history teacher in Grand Haven, Michigan, mentioned the Owen papers to Gordon Olson, the historian for the city of Grand Rapids, Michigan. Both men realized the importance of the papers, and Olson suggested that Owen's descendants, Shirley and Charles Millard, donate them to the Historical Division. They agreed, and the Historical Division, after seeing the papers, decided to publish them.

Between 8 April 1862 and 2 May 1865, Thomas Owen wrote the 55 letters that appear in this publication to his family in New York. In these letters, Owen often used the salutation "Dear Friends at Home," which the Historical Division chose for the title of this book. The collection of Owen's papers in the custody of the Historical Division includes some letters that he wrote long after the Civil War and others that he received from family and friends during the conflict. These few additional letters were not included because they add nothing to the story of Owen's role in the Civil War. Owen apparently wrote other letters home during the war, but the Historical Division has not located them.

The diary extends from 29 April to 18 May 1964. It covers the early stages of the Army of the Potomac's 1864 spring offensive. The Historical Division has not found any other diary entries.

The letters and diary were generally legible and easy to transcribe. In a few cases, however, including one soiled part of the diary, I could not transcribe some words. I have indicated these with blank underlined spaces.

Owen sometimes wrote in haste and made careless errors. In some instances, he left out words or suffixes. If I could not determine what the word or suffix was, I left a space which I framed in brackets. When I discovered what was missing, I included it in brackets. Also, Owen wrote some phrases or sentences and then drew lines through them. When possible and worthwhile, I transcribed these, and they appear with a line through them.

The diary and letters contained numerous spelling mistakes. Owen used "wer" for "were," "fer" for "for," and "verry" for "very." He misspelled many other words, particularly the names of people and places. Like most Civil War soldiers, he seldom saw the names of people or places in print. He usually heard them spoken and wrote the names phonetically. When Owen wrote "Johnson" for "Johnston," "Fort Steavenson," for "Fort Stevenson," and "Seymer" for "Seymour," he spelled them as well as he could. Although the various misspellings are interesting and sometimes humorous, for the sake of clarity I have corrected all of them.

Embossment on Thomas James Owen's stationery.

Generally, I have provided annotated footnotes for people and places mentioned in Owen's writings. For place names that appear in Dallas Irvine et al., *Military Operations of the Civil War: A Guide-Index to the Official Records of the Union and Confederate Armies, 1861–1865* (Washington, DC: Government Printing Office, 1968–1980); in the indexes to the War Department's *Atlas to Accompany the Official Records of the Union and Confederate Armies* (Washington, DC: Government Printing Office, 1891–1895); or in the *Rand McNally Cosmopolitan World Atlas* (Chicago: Rand McNally and Company, 1971), I refer the reader to the appropriate pages of these publications for information. In some cases I have provided additional information pertaining to the events, operations, and experiences that Owen described.

Like numerous Civil War soldiers who wrote letters and diaries, Owen simply jotted down his thoughts on paper. For readability, I have arranged the resultant phrases in sentences and paragraphs. Throughout his writings, Owen underlined certain words and included others in parentheses. I have left those as I found them. However, I have substituted "and" for ampersands (&) and corrected unwarranted capitalization. Although Owen used the contemporary term "pontoon," I changed it to the modern usage of "ponton."

I received valuable advice and assistance from numerous individuals and institutions. John Greenwood, Chief of the Historical Division, enthusiastically endorsed the project and provided encouragement. Two colleagues, Paul K. Walker and Frank N. Schubert, helped me in various ways ranging from transcription of difficult words to moral support. Michael Musick, my former colleague at the National Archives and a dedicated Civil War scholar, generously assisted me in locating information for some of the annotations. Others who provided useful suggestions and information were John Y. Simon, editor of the *The Papers of Ulysses S. Grant*; William Lay, Jr., curator of the Tioga County Historical Society in Owego, New York; Gordon Olson, city historian of Grand Rapids, Michigan; Richard Sommers, archivist at the U.S. Army Military History Institute in Carlisle Barracks, Pennsylvania; and various historians of the National Park Service at the Fredericksburg-Spotsylvania and Petersburg National Military Parks.

Archivists Maida Loescher, Mike Musick, Elaine Everly, Charles Shaughanessy, and John Dwyer ably assisted me in locating documents in the National Archives. The staff of the Minnesota Historical Society searched the William Watts Folwell Papers and located important documents and photographs, including a picture of Owen. Employees of the Prints and Photographs Division of the Library of Congress helped me find many pertinent illustrations.

Shirley and Charles Millard, Paul Trap, and Gordon Olson arranged for the donation of the Thomas J. Owen Papers to the Historical Division. Without their help, publication of the Owen letters and diary would have been impossible.

INTRODUCTION

Reality dawned slowly in the North during the secession year of 1861. Three months after the South fired the opening shots of the Civil War at Fort Sumter, the United States still expected that one battle would destroy the rebellion. Consequently, the government augmented its inconsiderable Regular Army with only a small number of three-month volunteers. On 21 July 1861, Union forces met the Confederate foe at Manassas. The rebels sent them reeling back to Washington and awakened the North to its folly.[1]

On the next day, Congress authorized President Abraham Lincoln to accept 500,000 volunteers for three years' service. The northern states began enlisting and equipping the recruits, and Lincoln brought to Washington a promising young general officer, George B. McClellan, to train and organize the new troops into an effective fighting force. Patriotic fervor facilitated mobilization. Lawyers and businessmen as well as farmers and laborers scrambled to enlist.[2]

Among the thousands of men who responded to the call for volunteers was a gray-eyed, brown-haired, 19-year-old farmboy named Thomas James Owen. The five-foot eight-inch, fair-skinned son of Thomas and Almira Owen enlisted on 14 August 1861. Unlike most of his peers, Owen entered the service as a sergeant rather than as a private.[3]

Along with 44 men, including friends and neighbors, Owen enrolled in Captain E.R. Patten's company at Owego, Tioga County, New York, his hometown. Other men from various towns in New York and Pennsylvania also joined the company. By 24 August, the unit totaled 83. The company traveled to Elmira, just west of Owego, where it assembled with nine other companies to form Stuart's Independent Regiment.[4]

Governor Edwin D. Morgan of New York originally authorized Charles B. Stuart, formerly the state engineer and surveyor, to raise and command a regiment of infantry. While at Elmira, Colonel Stuart set about instructing his men and oversaw their muster into federal service by a Regular Army officer. At that point, Owen officially became a member of Company I, Fiftieth New York Volunteer Infantry Regiment.[5]

In late September 1861, the regiment went to Washington, D.C., by train. After a short stay in the capital, it moved to Hall's Hill in Virginia. Here the regiment underwent a drastic change. General McClellan, in desperate need of combat Engineers, detailed the Fiftieth New York to act as sappers, miners, and pontoniers. In reassigning the regiment, McClellan noted the "unusual number of sailors and mechanics" in the Fiftieth. Thus, the Fiftieth New York Volunteer Engineer Regiment, its official designation after 17 July 1862, had many new jobs to learn and perform, including laying ponton bridges, erecting field fortifications, and constructing roads.[6]

General Barton S. Alexander, first commander of the Volunteer Engineer Brigade. *Library of Congress photograph B812-9342.*

In late October 1861, the regiment returned to Washington. There it settled in at Camp Lesley, which eventually became known as the Washington Engineer Depot, about one-half mile north of the Navy Yard on the Anacostia River.[7] Soon afterward, the Fifteenth New York Volunteer Infantry Regiment, also detailed as combat Engineers, encamped nearby. These two regiments formed the Volunteer Engineer Brigade of the Army of the Potomac, commanded successively by Lieutenant Colonel Barton S. Alexander, Brigadier General Daniel P. Woodbury, and Brigadier General Henry W. Benham.

On the other side of the Navy Yard, the Regular Army's small Engineer force bivouacked near the Washington Arsenal, at the site of present-day Fort Lesley J. McNair. This Battalion of Engineers worked closely with the Volunteer Engineer Brigade throughout the war and for a brief time, from 20 April to 7 July 1863, was part of it. Together, these units constituted the entire permanent Engineer force of the Army of the Potomac and performed valuable service throughout the Civil War.[8]

Sergeant Owen was responsible for training the men under him and leading them on the march and in battle. He performed his duties well. In early 1863, he received a promotion to first sergeant, which made him the senior noncommissioned officer in his company. Later he became a commissioned officer, receiving a promotion to second lieutenant on 17 March 1864 and first lieutenant as of 15 October 1864. In addition, he served as acting assistant quartermaster for his unit from 12 July 1864 until 1 June 1865.[9]

Owen's letters and diary are a worthy contribution to the literature of the Civil War. Few published, firsthand accounts by Civil War Engineers exist, especially for units in the Army of the Potomac. Gilbert Thompson, a private and later a corporal in the Battalion of Engineers, wrote a history of his unit, which included a day-by-day account of operations. An enlisted man in the Fifteenth New York Volunteer Engineer Regiment, writing under the pseudonym Don Pedro Quarendo Reminisco, published a book of poetry about his war experiences. Wesley Brainerd, an officer in the Fiftieth New York Volunteer Engineer Regiment, penned an article on the laying of ponton bridges during the Fredericksburg campaign. Seven letters of Deloss S. Burton, an enlisted man in the Fiftieth, appeared in print recently. These are the only published, firsthand accounts pertaining to the Fiftieth.[10]

Owen's writings shed needed light on a relatively unknown and neglected aspect of the Civil War—combat engineering. The Fiftieth New York Volunteer Engineer Regiment participated in every major campaign of the Army of the Potomac from the Peninsula to Appomattox. Among its achievements were field fortifications at Yorktown and Petersburg; ponton bridges at Fredericksburg and in the Peninsula; Antietam, Gettysburg, and Wilderness-Spotsylvania campaigns; and corduroy roads in Virginia and Maryland. Also, Owen and some of his subordinates assisted Philip Sheridan on his expeditions to the Shenandoah Valley in

1864 and 1865.

Finally, Owen's jottings document his varied career. At first, he was a noncommissioned officer overseeing the actions of a squad of men. Later, as senior noncommissioned officer and commissioned lieutenant, he assisted in administering a company. During the last year of the Civil War, he was a staff officer and commanded a unit the size of a company during the absences of his superior. Few northern farmboys had similar experiences during the war.

Following the Civil War, Owen returned to Owego, but he left home in October 1865 and moved to Michigan. Settling in Big Rapids on the Muskegon River in the central part of the state, he worked as a clerk in a store and as a bookkeeper. Apparently, he also obtained employment in the lumber business. During his 25-year residency in Michigan, Owen and his wife Alice, also a New Yorker, had one child, Blanche, who was born about 1875.[11]

In 1890, Owen moved to a farm outside Rhinelander, in north central Wisconsin. Engaged in farming for the rest of his life, Owen also surveyed timberland for the U.S. government. Additionally, he estimated the value of lumber on land owned by various companies. In 1913, Owen attended the Fiftieth Anniversary Veterans Reunion at Gettysburg and visited Owego. Following his return to Rhinelander, he fell ill and, on 4 March 1915, entered the Northwestern Branch, National Home for Disabled Volunteer Soldiers, in Milwaukee, Wisconsin. On 7 April, he died of Bright's disease and a weak heart and was buried in the soldiers' home cemetery in Milwaukee.[12]

NOTES TO INTRODUCTION

1. Francis F. Wilshin, *Manassas (Bull Run) National Battlefield Park, Virginia* (Washington, DC: Government Printing Office, 1953), pp. 5-6 and 16-18; James G. Randall and David Donald, *The Civil War and Reconstruction* (Second Edition, Revised, Lexington, Massachusetts: D.C. Heath and Company, 1969), pp. 192, 199-200, and 230; and Marvin A. Kreidberg and Merton G. Henry, *History of Military Mobilization in the United States Army 1775-1945* (Washington, DC: Government Printing Office, 1953), pp. 92-100.

2. Leonard L. Lerwill, *The Personnel Replacement System in the United States Army* (Washington, DC: Government Printing Office, 1954), p. 73; Kreidberg and Henry, *Military Mobilization*, pp. 93-94 and 97-98; Wilshin, *Manassas (Bull Run)*, p. 18; and War Department, *The War of the Rebellion: A Compilation of the Official Records of the Union and Confederate Armies* (Washington, DC: Government Printing Office, 1880-1901) (hereafter referred to as *Official Records, Army*), Series I, Volume 2, p. 753.

3. No explanation of Owen's enlistment as a sergeant while others became privates was found. Thomas J. Owen, Compiled Military Service Record, Fiftieth New York Volunteer Engineer Regiment, Carded Records, Volunteer Organizations: Civil War (hereafter referred to as Owen, CMSR), Record Group 94, Records of the Adjutant General's Office National Archives Building (hereafter referred to as RG 94); Thomas J. Owen, C2533270, Military Service Pension Application Files, 1861-1934 (hereafter referred to as Owen, Pension), Record Group 15, Records of the Veterans Administration National Archives Building (hereafter referred to as RG 15); Numbers 5-8, p. 257, Owego, Roll 604, Microcopy 432, *Seventh Census of the United States, 1850*, and Numbers 27-31, p. 402, Owego, Roll 867, Microcopy 653, *Eighth Census of the United States, 1860*, both in Record Group 29, Records of the Bureau of the Census, National Archives Building (hereafter referred to as RG 29); and Kreidberg and Henry, *Military Mobilization*, p. 98.

4. New York Adjutant General's Office, *A Record of the Commissioned Officers, Noncommissioned Officers and Privates of the Regiments Which Were Organized in the State of New York. . .* (Albany: Comstock and Cassidy Printers, 1864), Volume 2, p. 328; New York State Monuments Commission for the Battlefields of Gettysburg and Chattanooga, *Final Report on the Battlefield of Gettysburg* (Albany: J.B. Lyon Company, 1902) (hereafter referred to as NYSMC, *Final Report*), Volume 3, p. 1090; Frederick Phisterer, compiler, *New York in the War of the Rebellion 1861 to 1865* (Albany: J.B. Lyon Company, 1912), pp. 1669-1670; Thomas E. Byrne, "Elmira, 1861-1865: Civil War Rendezvous," *Chemung Historical Journal* 9 (June 1964), pp. 1247-1252; and General Order No. 58, Adjutant General's Office, 15 August 1861, Order and Circulars, 1797-1910 (hereafter referred to as O&C), RG 94.

5. NYSMC, *Final Report*, Volume 3, pp. 1090-1091; Kreidberg and Henry, *Military Mobilization*, p. 98; Byrne, "Elmira, 1861-1865," pp. 1247-1252;

Dumas Malone, ed., "Charles Beebe Stuart," *Dictionary of America Biography* (New York: Charles Scribner's Sons, 1936), Volume 18, p. 163; "Very Rough Outline of History of 50th N.Y. Engineers, Made August 1911," in the William Watts Folwell Papers, Minnesota Historical Society (hereafter referred to as "Rough History," Folwell Papers, MHS), p. 4; and General Order No. 58, Adjutant General's Office, 15 August 1861, O&C, and Record of Events Cards (hereafter referred to as REC), Regimental Return, August 1861, Fiftieth New York Volunteer Engineer Regiment, Roll 136, Microcopy 594, *Compiled Records Showing Service of Military Units in Volunteer Union Organizations* (hereafter referred to as M594), RG 94.

6. "Rough History," Folwell Papers, MHS, pp. 4–5; *U.S. Statutes at Large* 597 (Section 20); George B. McClellan, *McClellan's Own Story* (New York: Charles L. Webster and Company, 1887), p. 119; *The Union Army...* (Madison, Wisconsin: Federal Publishing Company, 1908), Volume 2, pp. 86–87; NYSMC, *Final Report*, Volume 3, p. 1091; *Official Records, Army, Series I*, Volume 5, pp. 24–25, and Volume 6, pp. 172–173, and Series III, Volume 1, p. 534; Phillip M. Thienel, "Engineers in the Union Army, 1861–1865," *The Military Engineer* 47 (January–February 1955), pp. 36–38; REC, Regimental Return, October 1861, Fiftieth New York Volunteer Engineer Regiment, Roll 136, M594, RG 94; and Paragraph 15, Special Order No. 113, Army of the Potomac, 22 October 1861, Volume 27AP, p. 215 (hereafter referred to as SO 113, A of P), Special Orders, Army of the Potomac (hereafter referred to as SOs, A of P), Record Group 393, Records of United States Army Continental Commands, 1821–1920, National Archives Building (hereafter referred to as RD 393).

7. SO 113, A of P, and SOs, A of P, RG 393. Some authors have stated that the Volunteer Engineer Brigade Depot or Washington Engineer Depot was near the Engineer Battalion Headquarters at the foot of 4½ Street, SW. See Engineer School, *History and Traditions of the Corps* (Fort Belvoir, Virginia: Engineer School Press, 1953), p. 29; and Warren T. Hannum, "The Crossing of the James River 1864," *The Military Engineer* 15 (May–June 1923), p. 232. Actually, Camp Lesley/Washington Engineer Depot was "one-half mile above the U.S. Navy Yard" and "on the right bank of the Eastern branch of the Potomac" (Anacostia), probably at the foot of East 14th and/or 15th Streets. See "Rough History," Folwell Papers, MHS, p. 5; Chief of Engineers to Henry W. Benham, 25 November 1863, Volume 36, p. 164, Letters Sent to Engineer Officers, Record Group 77, Records of the Office of the Chief of Engineers, National Archives Building; Daniel P. Woodbury to George Ford, 3 September 1862, Volume 52/117AP, Letters Sent, Engineer Brigade, Army of the Potomac, RG 393; and *Official Records Army*, Series I, Volume 29, Part II, pp. 462–467.

8. Gilbert Thompson, *The Engineer Battalion in the Civil War*, Occasional Papers No. 44 (Washington Barracks, DC: Press of the Engineer School, 1910), pp. 1–4 and 100; G.A. Youngberg, *History of Engineer Troops in the United States Army 1775–1901*, Occasional Papers No. 37 (Washington Barracks, DC: Press of the Engineer School, 1910), pp. 63–70; Thienel, "Engineers in the Union Army," p. 38; *Official Records Army*, Series I, Volume 2, Part I, p. 36, and Part II, p. 108, and Volume 25, Part II, p. 150, and Volume 51,

Part I, p. 497; NYSMC, *Final Report*, Volume 3, p. 1091; "Rough History," Folwell Papers, MHS, pp. 4-5; and Paragraph 7, Special Order No. 122, Army of the Potomac, 29 October 1861, p. 235, and Paragraph 19, Special Order No. 61, Army of the Potomac, 3 March 1862, p. 585, both in Volume 27AP, and Paragraph 5, Special Order No. 108, Army of the Potomac, 20 April 1863, page 274, and paragraph 2, Special Order No. 182, Army of the Potomac, 7 July 1863, p. 400, both in Volume 29AP, SOs, A of P, RG 393.

9. Owen, CMSR, and 13015 VS 1865, Letters Received, Volunteer Service Division (hereafter referred to as LR, VSD), RG 94.

10. Gilbert Thompson, *The Engineer Battalion*; Don Pedro Quarendo Reminisco, *Life in the Union Army; or, Notings and Reminiscences of a Two Years' Volunteer* (New York: H. Dexter, Hamilton and Company, 1863); Wesley Brainerd, "The Pontoniers at Fredericksburg," in Robert U. Johnson and Clarence Buel, eds., *Battles and Leaders of the Civil War*, 4 Volumes (New York: Century Company, 1887-1888), Volume 3, pp. 121-122; Charles E. Dornbusch, compiler, *Military Bibliography of the Civil War* (New York: New York Public Library, 1961-1972), Volume 1, pp. 23-29, Volume 2, pp. 35, 63-64, 143, and 157, and Volume 3, page 61; and Deloss S. Burton, "Spotsylvania: Letters From The Field; An Eyewitness," *Civil War Times Illustrated* 22 (April 1983), pp. 22-27.

11. Owen, Pension, RG 15; Numbers 12 and 13, p. 1, Michigan, Mecosta County, Big Rapids, First Ward, Roll 690, Microcopy 593, *Ninth Census of the United States, 1870*, and Numbers 13-15, p. 16, Michigan, Mecosta County, Big Rapids, First Ward, Roll 594, Microcopy T-9, *Tenth Census of the United States, 1880*, RG 29; and Obituary, *Owego Gazette*, 22 April 1915.

12. Obituary, *Owego Gazette*, 22 April 1915; Owen, Pension, RG 29; and 3015 VS 1865, LS, VSD, RG 94.

Thomas Owen's Letters
8 April 1862 – 2 May 1865

1.   Alexandria, Virginia, April 8th, 1862

Dear Friends at Home,[1]

Once more I have the pleasure of writing to you. I received yours before we left Camp Woodbury.[2] I will now try and give you a description or history of our journey which commenced on Friday last.

Last Friday morn about 2 A.M. o'clock we were awoke by the drums, and the cooks were ordered to cook 3 days' rations before morning, as we were ordered to Manassas at 5 o'clock. Well, 5 o'clock came but we did not start until 1 P.M. We then went to the railroad to take the cars for Manassas, but as the 15th [New York Volunteer Engineer Regiment] was ahead of us and there being a lack of cars, we were obliged to wait until morning before we could go. So we stuck up our little tents. I laid down to rest.

In the morning, we found the weather bad, for it rained quite hard, but we could not stop for rain. So we went to work and packed our knapsacks so as to be ready when the train came along. We were ready long before the train came.

At last it came, and about 11½ A.M. o'clock we started for Manassas, where we arrived about 2½ o'clock P.M. We rode in open cars, and therefore we had a good chance to see the country; and a rough sight it is. On our way we crossed Bull Run Creek, and from there to Manassas and on beyond is [sic] the worst sights I ever saw. Around the Junction,[3] as you must know, the rebels destroyed a great quantity of stuff just before they left, the ruins of which can be plainly seen still. There are also a great many rebel camps still standing, some of which are occupied by our troops. I saw in one place, along the track at Manassas, where the rebels had burnt a lot of cars with all their contents which appeared to have been trunks. In another place was a large pile of wagon iron which showed that wagons had there been burnt. Hundreds of dead horses lay scattered all around. I cannot tell you all that I saw there now.

We pitched our camp about 2 miles beyond Manassas, where we stayed two nights and a little over one day. While there, I went around some but not as much as I would like to, on account of our short stay.

I was into several rebel camps. They seem to have had good quarters this last winter. They did not live in tents but they built log huts, some of which were very nice. There was one camp near where we stopped, and you had ought to have seen the boys. Soon after we got there every man seemed to be bringing something into camp. Some had pots, some beds, boards, chairs, old bayonets, and in fact everything that they could find that had belonged to the rebels.

Sunday was a fine day, and just at night we got orders to march the next morn at 7 A.M. o'clock for the Rappahannock River. Well, we started at the appointed time and marched about 5 miles when an order came for us (that is, the 50th and 15th Regiments) to turn back, for we were ordered to Fortress Monroe.[4] We then marched back to Manassas where we were to take the cars for Alexandria. The 15th marched before us and so they were loaded first.

About 2 o'clock P.M. it commenced to snow, and Colonel Murphy[5] said we should all have covered cars, and so we waited until almost dark before we got on. I must say that I had a pretty hard time that afternoon and night. Thank God we got covered cars, but the train was so heavy that the engine could take us but 5 miles when it had to leave part of us and go on with what it could draw, and there we sat in the cars all night. I can say for myself that I did not sleep a wink.

In the morning an engine came and took us on, and we arrived here about noon, cold and hungry, and when we started we only took one meal in our haversacks. We expect to go on board [a steamer] in the morning and then away for Fortress Monroe.[6]

The 15th have gone on board tonight. It is now after 10 o'clock P.M. and I am quite sleepy. Our company is quartered in a hall tonight. The boys have all laid down on the floor and I can tell by the breathing that they sleep.

I hope you will write soon. Most likely I cannot in some time.

                         Goodbye from your son

[On back of letter] I will write and let you know where I am, if I can, after we move. My health is good. Give my respects to all. Tell Putt⁷ that I have not forgotten him.

Goodbye from Tommy

2.

Yorktown, Virginia
August 18th, 1862

Dear Friends at Home,

    Having a few moments to spare, I will let you know where I am. The first thing is, I am well. We left Harrison's Landing,[1] on the morning of the 13th for parts unknown to us. Our knapsacks were put on board the transports. We had our tents, rubber blankets, and woolen blankets to carry. Well, about 8 A.M. we started, 3 days' rations in our haversacks, and all armed with either axes, picks, or shovels besides our guns. We took a southeast course down the James. Passed our pickets about 10 A.M. There were four companies of us in all; they were B, G, K, and I. We were then on our own hooks. I have not time to tell you all about the march now.

    We stopped at Charles City Court House long enough to eat dinner at that place. We captured a young Cesesh[2] with a team [and] a wagon who we made draw our tools. I've lots of things to tell but I can't now.

    Arrived at the mouth of the Chickahominy about noon of the 14th. Started on the 15th for Williamsburg. Arrived there at night and stayed until morning. Arrived at Yorktown on the eve, on the 16th, where we remain for orders. There is [sic] only 2 companies of us here. The other 2 remained at the Chickahominy. The whole army is coming down. I hear that Pope had a big fight.[3] This is all at present.

    I am the only sergeant able for duty, and the only one with the company. I received the *Frank Leslies*[4] you sent.

    Those mortars look just as natural as life.

    This is all. Please to write soon.

                  Your affectionate son

                  Sergeant Thomas J. Owen
                  Company I, 50th New York State Volunteer Engineers

3.
                                    Camp of Engineer Detachment
                                    Near Falmouth[, Virginia]
                                    January 13th, 1863

Dear Friends at Home,

    I received yours of the 6th this eve from Alice and was much pleased to hear that you had received the present I sent you. I hope you will put it to good use. You must take pains when you write, and soon you will be a good writer.

    We are now in a fine place. It is in a pine woods. We have built up our tents with logs so that they are very nice and warm. The weather is fine for the time of the year. Think some of moving soon, which don't please us much now that we have such a nice place. The company is quite well at present.

    You must improve your time at school as best you can, for your education is something that will be of great service to you yet, if you live.

    I want to hear quite often how you are getting along. I am in such a hurry that I have not time to write much more. I hope to hear from this soon. From your affectionate brother,

                                      Thomas

4.
                                        Camp Engineer Corps
                                        Near Stoneman Station,[1] Virginia
                                        February 2d, 1863

Dear Friends at Home,

    I have a few spare moments which I will try and improve. I received yours of the 23d January a few days since and have not had a chance to answer it until now. I have not much news about the war.

    Philip R. Goodrich[2] has been promoted to 2d lieutenant of our company. He received his commission yesterday. I have been appointed orderly[3] of said company. For my part, I am glad to see Phil get up. I think he has been skipped to[o] long. The company is in quite good health. We have had some snow lately but it is about gone now. I am at a loss to think what the Army will do next. I hardly think Joe[4] will make another push for Richmond this winter. If he does, I hope he will meet with better success than Burnside[5] did. The Army is getting a little discouraged, I think, but not half so much as people at the North think. Just send Little Mac[6] down here to lead us and then you will see what we are. The mud is drying up some. I have not much more time now. Please to send the papers every week.

    My respects to all, your affectionate son,

                                                      Orderly Sergeant Thomas J. Owen

5.　　　　　　　　　　Camp of Detachment
　　　　　　　　　　　50th New York Volunteer Engineers
　　　　　　　　　　　near Falmouth, Virginia
　　　　　　　　　　　May 21st, 1863

Dear Father and Friends at Home,

　　Several days have passed since I received your letter of the 8th, and I have been waiting for something of importance to turn up so that I could have something of interest to write you, but I guess I shall have to wait sometime for that. Nearly all I can say now is that I am well.

　　Day before yesterday the colonel called me to his tent and told me that he would like to have me go with an artist to the river and point out the spot where Captain Perkins[1] was shot. I told him it would please me much to do so.

Sketch of Engineer troops laying ponton bridge at Fredericksburg, Virginia, 11 December 1862, by Alfred R. Waud. *Library of Congress photograph Z62-7023.*

At one o'clock the artist called for me and we started, having been furnished with a pass from General Hooker to go outside the picket lines. 2 o'clock found us at the spot. Yes, there was the spot where fell a noble man, and there were the old houses where the sharpshooters concealed themselves while firing at us, and there was the famous Rappahannock moving slowly along towards the bay, the same as ever. Oh, how fresh. It brought the scene of battle back to me. There also was the place where poor Champlin[2] fell just as he had reached the opposite shore. All these things flashed through my mind in a moment as I stood gazing at the old city.[3]

May 22d. I did not have time to finish this last eve so I will continue this morning. The rebels now occupy the city. Their pickets were along the opposite bank not more than 400 feet from the spot where Captain Perkins fell. I went to the very spot. We then retired to the top of the bank and the artist proceeded to take the sketch which is to be sent to Captain Perkins' brother in New York. We were there until 4½ o'clock. All the while we were there the rebs were drilling. Just back of the city we could see them very plain. While the artist was sketching, I also took a sketch of the buildings that stand close to the bank on the opposite side. I will finish it up and send it home.

The scenery about Fredericksburg is very fine, and in time of place it must have been a pleasant place to live in. Yesterday, we had a General Review by General Benham.[4] The prospects for a move are not as bright as they were a short time since. I can form no idea of what is to be done. I must now close. Please tell me who you let [lent?] the money to.

                        I remain your affectionate son,
                        Thomas J. Owen

6.   Camp of 50th New York Volunteer Engineers
near Falmouth, Virginia
June 6th, 1863

Dear Father and Friends at Home,

I take this early opportunity of letting you know that I am still alive and well. You will see that I wrote you yesterday morning. Also sent you some money. You also remember that I told you we had orders to go and lay a bridge. Well, the bridge is laid, and we now hold the opposite side of the Rappahannock, but we did not gain it without shedding blood. Let me give you the events as they occurred.

They are as follows.[1]

At about 8 o'clock we received orders to get ready to move the train to the river. Soon after, we received orders to move, and in about 2 hours from the time we received orders to get ready, we were at the river with our train.

We then waited until about 4 o'clock before the troops came that were going to cross. In meantime, we amused ourselves looking at the Johnnys[2] on the other side. They had a fine rifle pit, and we knew that they would give us trouble. The day was quite warm, and at length we began to grow anxious for the fun to commence. A little after 4, the artillery began to wheel into position, and we could see the rebs coming from other points to strengthen the point opposite where we were to cross, which was about 2 miles below the city of Fredericksburg. At 5¼ o'clock, the first gun was fired which was from our artillery aimed at some skirmishers that were coming up from below. Oh, I never shall forget that scene. I think it was one of the grandest scenes I every saw. I was where I had a good view of the whole thing. First came the boom of the gun, and the next instance the balls were skipping away over the level plain (which extends over a mile back from the river), carrying death and destruction with them.

At 6½ o'clock we started down to the water with the pontons,[3] the object being to throw infantry across in boats and drive them out of their rifle pits. Although our artillery kept up a continual firing, they did not hinder the enemy from keeping up a brisk fire of musketry at us. As we marched down the bank, the ball fell thick and fast around. Now and then some poor fellow would drop with a cry of pain on his lips.

When we got down the bank we had orders to lay down. The most of the boys did so. Now and then we would get up and unload a boat. At length we had 10 boats unloaded. Captain Folwell[4] then came and asked me to go up the hill after the boatmen who were to ferry the infantry over. I started and just as I got to the top of

Captain, later Major, William Watts Folwell commanded Company I, Fiftieth New York Volunteer Engineer Regiment. *William Watts Folwell Collection photograph CN#11, Minnesota Historical Society.*

the hill, I looked around and saw a little curl of white smoke rise from the center of the pit, and the next instant, a minie[5] whizzed close to me. I went on, and before I had taken 5 steps, 3 more struck the ground just ahead of me. I then took a zigzag course so they could not aim at me, and went on. I have reason to think that all four balls were aimed at me, for there was no one else within 10 rods of where I was. Well, I found the boatmen and then I soon went back and helped ferry the first regiment over. As soon as the infantry took the works, the firing ceased and then we went to work, and soon the Rappahannock was bridged and once more General Sedgwick[6] was crossing over. Our whole brigade was there, general and all, but Companies A, F, and I layed the bridge, which constitutes Major Spaulding's[7] detachment. As a general thing the boys did well. ~~we only had one sneak in our Company and he was a new man, one of the recruits that came last fall his name~~. Corporal Armstrong[8] of our company was the only man hurt. He was wounded in the foot somewhere about the heel but I think not dangerously. Our regiment lost (as far as I know of now) 10 wounded and one killed besides one officer wounded, Lieutenant Newcome[9] of Company C, in head.

I think the main part of the enemy's force has left for some other parts unknown to us here. The main part of the Army of the Potomac is also gone. I think Joe is enough for the Johnnys. Very likely, you know more about the Army than I do.

We can hear some firing today. The weather is fine. It is now almost time for the mail to leave. I will have to cut short with a goodbye to you all. I remain with a whole hide, your affectionate son,

        Thomas J. Owen
        Orderly Company I,
        50th New York Volunteer Engineers

7.   Camp of 50th New York Volunteer Engineers
          Washington, D.C.
          July 6th, 1863

Dear Friends at Home,

I now have about 5 minutes which I will spend in writing. We are now camped in the old ground[1] in Washington.

Came here on the night of the 3d having had a long and tiresome march from Edwards Ferry via Frederick City, Johnsville, Liberty [now Libertytown], New Market, and so around to Washington. Were on the march almost day and night for 6 days. When we came in here we were footsore and nearly tired out.[2] We only had 2 days rations out of the 6, but the people along the way gave us plenty to eat. Oh, how I want to tell you all about the march, but I have not time now. I began a letter yesterday and was going to give you a full detail of the whole thing but this morning we have orders to pack up. The report is that Companies I and H go to Harpers Ferry. The boys are packing up now. I have packed and thus I have time to write this hasty note. I am well.

While we were out, we had some pretty narrow escapes from the rebs cavalry, but we came out all right. The whole train was saved. I hope you enjoyed the 4th. I can't say I did. I must stop now or I'll be behind. Don't fail to write soon.

I have received several letters from you. I received one from Ely[3] and Alice a day or two since. Our mail has been very irregular. We have been twice, 5 or 6 days without mail but at last it came in a heap. I hear we have no more Longstreet.[4] Goodbye. Look out to hear from me again before long.

Your affectionate son,

Thomas J. Owen

P.S. Respects to all. Tell them I am well.

Thomas

8.   Camp of 50th New York Volunteer Engineers
Washington, D.C.
August 2d, 1863

Dear Father and Friends at Home,

Your kind letter of the 31st came to hand this P.M. and now I will immediately let you know how and where I am. You see by the heading that we are now in Washington. We came here on the 29th from Berlin which we left the 27th, having taken up our bridge ere we started. Our trip down the canal was a fine one though at the latter end I met with a misfortune as follows:[1]

At Georgetown we left the main canal and struck off into the old canal,[2] which by the way is not in use nor has it been for sometime past. Well, while we were getting through with our train, we came to a [place] where the water was very shallow, and our timber raft stuck.

I, of course, was soon in the water lifting and tugging to get off, little thinking then what was to follow. At length we got off and in due time arrived in camp. By this time, my feet began to burn and pain me severely. This was about 3 P.M., and so they continued until about midnight when I managed to stop the burning, but man they were so swollen that it was impossible for me to use them. I have been off duty ever since. They are better today so that I have on my shoes and stockings. I shall go on duty tomorrow. I think my feet were poisoned by gas, tar, etc., that runs into the old canal, the bottom being full of it. Several other of the boys also got a dose; but none so bad as myself. The prospects are that we will stay here sometime.

Sergeant LaGrange[3] has gone to Elmira after conscripts.

The health of the company is good.

Weather very warm.

The draft takes place here tomorrow. Some talk of our being called out to patrol the city and keep peace.[4]

Some talk of a mob.

I must close now.

I remain your son, etc.,

                    Thomas J. Owen

9.   Camp of 50th New York Volunteer Engineers
               Washington, D.C.
               August 15th, 1863

Dear Father and Friends at Home,

    We have just received two months' pay and now I take the earliest opportunity of sending to you my allotment, as usual $20.00.
    The weather is very warm. We are quite healthy considering. I have little as no news at present. I hear that the conscripts are paying their little [$]300.[1] Well, they must want to stay at home more than I do. For my part, I would not give 10 cents to stay at home, if I was there that is, as long as the war lasts.
    I have not time to write a long letter now, so please excuse me and remember me as your affectionate son,

        Thomas J. Owen

P.S. I also send you my photograph that I had taken a few days since. It is rather dark but it is as good as I can get now.

        Thomas

10.
                                                        Washington, D.C.
                                                        August 22d, 1863

Dear Father and Sister Alice,

    I have just received both your kind letters bearing date August 20th, and indeed, I was very glad to hear from you. You spoke about receiving the money but not a word did you say about my picture. How did you like it anyhow? You also spoke about cousin Lucretia.[1] I am glad you are going to let her know where I am, and I hope to hear from her myself before long. Please tell her to write to me and I will answer.

    I see you meant to send your letter by George Forsyth[2] but he gave you the slip. He came here yesterday about noon. I was very much pleased to see him as he was just from home. He said he saw you the day before.

    We still remain in the city. The weather is very warm but we do not have to work very hard. The most of my duty is in the morning and evening but I have to be on hand all the while. The health of the company is good. I never felt better. On the 20th, we drew linen trousers which are much better this warm weather than the common woolen.

    There is little of interest going on now here. I see the news from Charleston[3] is good, and I sincerely hope that this nest of rebels may be cleaned out and receive a punishment due them for opening this wicked war.[4] But, we have not much to brag of, for in our own native state, yes in the noble Empire State, they have been guilty of as base an act as the citizens of Charleston.[5] In either place, they are guilty of treason, and I sincerely hope they may meet with a just punishment either in this world or the next. I suppose the drafted about Owego are mostly paying their $300.00. Well, I pity them. Before I would be such a coward, I would come, [even?] if I was sure of being shot. Of course, I do not say that all are cowards that pay, but there are those that dare not come, dare not serve the country that sustains them, the Government that protects them. But, I think I will close.

    I wish Alice to let me know how she is getting along, what she is studying, and where she is in her books, etc.

    With love and respect for you all, I remain as ever your son and brother,

                                                               Thomas J. Owen

11.   Camp of 50th New York Volunteer Engineers
                 Rappahannock Station, Virginia
                 September 27th, 1863

Dear Friends at Home,

Once more we are in the field. We left Washington on Wednesday the 23d, about 3 P.M., and marched into Virginia. Camped about 8 o'clock near Balls Crossroads and about 1½ miles from Uptons Hill. The 24th we lay still until 2 P.M. and then took up the line of march to Fairfax Station where we stopped at 9 P.M. The 25th we broke camp at 8 A.M., marched through Fairfax and turned about and went back to where we stopped during the night. There we waited until about noon for a portion of the 11th Corps[1] that were on their way to Tennessee. We then marched to Bull Run where we stopped for the night. 26th broke camp at 7 A.M. and marched to Warrenton Junction where we stayed all night. Today we marched to this place. We came here about noon, have not put [up] our tents yet for we know not whether we will stay here or not.

The weather has been fine so far. We have not put up our tents since we started. I have stood the march well. Some of the boys have sore feet.

The Army has advanced from here.

I think that I never saw such a desolate looking country as that which we have just passed through from Long Bridge to this place. There is scarcely a fence and but few houses, except in the villages, and they look mighty desolate. As for the cultivation, there is none; hardly a hill of corn is growing between here and the Capitol. On our way we passed through Fairfax, Centreville, Manassas, Bristoe Station, Catlet's Station, Warrenton Junction, Bealton, and last, Rappahannock Station. Here we are close to the old river on which we have seen so much service. The prospects are that we will go on to the front soon. The Regulars have gone on today. There is a bridge here that one of our companies laid sometime ago. I saw some of the 137th [New York Infantry Regiment][2] today. They say they are going to Tennessee. They belong to the 12th Corps.[3]

A[s] for war news, I have none. Please don't fail to send me the Owego papers. I am expecting to hear from you by the next mail as we have not had any since the 23d. I will now close. Please give my respects to all inquiring friends. I remain your affectionate son,

                    Thomas J.

12.
                        Camp of Detachment
                        50th New York Volunteer Engineers
                        Rappahannock Station, Virginia
                        December 8th, 1863

The victim of [a] melancholy accident was one of my most intimate friends. I became acquainted with him during the spring of 1856. From that time until he enlisted (1861) we were warm friends, always together whenever it was practicable, and while in the service we corresponde[d] with each other. And during our long acquaintance we never quarreled or passed an angry word with each other. I feel that I have lost a noble friend and one whom I can never forget. In the midst of dangers have I been spared while my most intimate acquaintances have been cut off in the mids[t] of civil life. But he on whose footstool we dwell does decide, and we poor mortals must abide.

                        Thomas J. Owen, Company I
                        50th New York Volunteer Engineers

This happened on the 20th of November 1863.

[Newspaper Obituary]

Killed Instantly

John Frear,[1] son of Mr. John Frear, who resides about two miles east of Owego village, was killed on the track of the Erie Railway early on Friday morning of last week. His body was literally torn to pieces and scattered along the track.

How this melancholy accident occurred we cannot tell. It appears by the statement of his father, that he left home about 4½ o'clock, on Friday morning, intending to go down the river on a raft or ark, which was lying near the residence of Mr. Leonard. Those living in that locality, when the going is bad, usually walk to town on the track, but how the accident could have occurred no one knows. A young, active, healthy man in the prime of life, could hardly permit himself to be run over, no matter in what way the train was moving. There are suspicions that he may have met with foul play and may have been laid on the track. John Frear was a fine quiet young man, much estimated and highly respected, and his unfortunate end has brought sorrow to the hearts of one of our most respectable families.

The following from those who served with him on the tented field will show their estimate of his worth both as a man and as a soldier:

The victim of this melancholy accident was among the first to respond to the call of his country. In the spring of the year 1861 he volunteered in H Co. 3d Infantry N.Y.V. and served for two years, the term of his enlistment, with credit to himself and his country. Always ready as he was to obey the call of duty, kind, obliging and genial, he was ever a favorite in his company and regiment; and his loss will deeply be regretted by his old associates in arms.

After passing through the dangers and privations incident to camp life, it seems sad to have him thus cut off in the midst of his days.

To his afflicted friends who have thus been called to mourn the loss of a kind and obedient son and affectionate brother, we offer our heartfelt sympathies.

May he who afflicteth not willingly console them in this sad bereavement.

Members of H Co. 3d N.Y.V.

13.	Camp of 50th New York Volunteer Engineers
Rappahannock Station, Virginia
December 19th, 1863

Dear Father and Friends at Home,

Your kind and welcome letter came to hand this evening. I was much pleased to hear from you but was a little surprised to learn that you have not heard from me since I sent my allotment, for I assure you I have written since and was expecting an answer.

There is little news as to the Army other than what you have ere this heard. We are fixing up good winter quarters. I think the plan now is to stay here this winter. Still, we cannot tell. Time works wonderful changes.

At present, I am on duty on the road between here and Bealton which a large number of infantry are repairing by building corduroy bridges,[1] etc. Captain Folwell has charge of the whole detail, and I go out to superintend certain jobs which they will not do well if they are not watched. I like General Meade's[2] plan of fixing the roads. It gives him a great advantage on the move, especially if it is in a wet time.

Sunday December 20th. I did not have time to finish this last night. Today, we are not busy at anything in particular. As usual, we are trying to observe the Sabbath.

What is your opinion about the war? I do not think it can last a great while longer by what we see in the papers. The South are [sic] getting sick of the job. Of late, we have been victorious both at the ballot box and in the field of mortal combat. All go to show that the North is bound to sustain the Union.

You undoubtedly expect me home next summer, but if the war is not over, it is doubtful whether you will see me then; but I do not say that you may not see me before that time.

The weather is cool, though not more so than we expect this season of the year. We shall look forward for some recruits before long—either volunteers or conscripts. I presume the poor fools up north are trembling in their boots, thinking of the 5th January and the terrible Draft,[3] poor fellows. I pity them, especially if they are situated so that they cannot leave home, and more so if they have not heart enough to fight for the Government that has protected them thus long. It is the latter class that cannot appreciate the blessings of this noble republic. They are wrapped up within themselves and care not how humanity progresses, so long as they enjoy freedom and the blessings somebody else has won for them. I have not time to say more on this subject, if I cared to. I am well, and we are all in fine spirits.

Hoping to again hear from you soon, I remain your affectionate son,

Thomas J. Owen

Engineer troops building corduroy road, Richmond, Virginia, June 1862. *Library of Congress photograph B8171-656.*

14.

Camp of Detachment
50th New York Volunteer Engineers
Rappahannock Station, Virginia
February 5th, 1864

Dear Father,

Again I find myself in my tent sitting by a comfortable fire which is blazing away in my new fireplace that the boys built for me while I was home.

I tell you it seemed good to me to get back again and meet the happy smiles and the warm shake of the hand from my noble boys.[1] I was much pleased to find the company in so fine a condition, not a man sick, all feeling finely. Indeed it takes away the dread of a soldier's life to have good men with him. Men that one can feel towards as he would towards a brother. Well, I left the famed city Wednesday morning at 9:45 and arrived in camp at 3 P.M. We were a little behind time on our furloughs but nothing was said. I had a fine chat with Lieutenant Colonel Spaulding,[2] and he was much pleased to learn that we had a good visit. Likewise [he] expressed his satisfaction on seeing us return.

Well there, what do you think is on foot now? I will tell you. The Captain just called me to his tent and told me to have the company ready to march in the morning at eight o'clock. Bully for that. We report to General Newton[3] commanding the 1st Army Corps.[4] We know nothing more about it but suspect we shall cross the Rapidan before we come back. We go to Culpeper in the morn. This came a little unexpected but I am ready and willing to go. The weather is mild. The roads are not very muddy. I hope this will find you well. Hoping to hear from you and Alice soon.

I remain your,

Thomas

15.   Camp of Detachment
         50th New York Volunteer Engineers
         Rappahannock Station, Virginia
         February 14th, 1864

Dear Father and Friends at Home,

 Last night I received the first letter since my return. It was from you and Alice, having a date February 10th. It is indeed a pleasure to hear that mother is getting better. Tell her not to worry about me in the least for I am well and have comfortable quarters. Very good living. In fact, I am enjoying myself. The weather is mild though rather windy.

 Our late move did not amount to much as far as hardship is concerned. We went beyond Culpeper on Saturday the 6th where we stayed until Sunday afternoon and then started back to camp where we arrived Monday noon. So here we are all right.

 On the march we passed through Culpeper, a small town laying between the two rivers, Rappahannock and Rapidan, about midway, and is twenty-six miles north of Gordonsville and sixty-two west of Alexandria, is the county seat of Culpeper County and contained, before the war, about 1200 inhabitants, but since the war it has seen ill-usage and now shows marks of the rebellion. The country round about is rolling and very fertile, but now it presents a sorry sight. Scarcely a stick of fencing is visible while most of the Lords of Creation[1] have fled to parts more undisturbed by war.

 Today is Sunday. We have had our inspection of arms, likewise of tents. Found everything in good condition. The company is well and contains, in all, 101 men, 80 which are present. The twenty-two [sic] are on detach[ed] service, absent with leave, sick, etc. Things are very quiet in camp. Today there is no work going on and the men show respect for the Sabbath by refraining from the usual sports. As we have no chaplain[2] with us we cannot attend divine service. Still, there are other ways by which we can respect this holy day. There is little news now. The whole Army seems to be enjoying winter quarters. The other day I went to Army Headquarters on business for the company. The camp is about 5 miles from here and about two miles from Brandy Station (northeast), situated in a piece of pine woods on a slight eminence, and for miles around towering above the treetops can be seen the beautiful emblem of the Union.[3] The grounds are in fine condition. The tents

Winter camp, Fiftieth New York Volunteer Engineer Regiment, Rappahannock, Virginia, March 1864. *Library of Congress photograph.*

Entrance to camp of Fiftieth New York Volunteer Engineer Regiment, Rappahannock Station, Virginia, March 1864. *Library of Congress photograph 351.*

stand in the shape of a half moon, General Meade's in the center. I will now close. Hoping this finds you all well.

I remain your son,

Thomas

P.S. I enclose a photograph of one of my boys, John H. Bunzey,[4] for Alice's album.

Thomas

16.   Rappahannock Station, Virginia
                              February 20th, 1864

Dear Father and Friends at Home,

    The mail this afternoon brought me a letter from you dated 17th, and I will not keep you in long suspense before you hear from me. Now, do not make up your minds that you are about to hear of some wonderful event, for if you do, you will suffer a disappointment.

    Indeed, there is little going on now save the old routine of camp duty which is always nearly the same, but when there is not too much of it, all goes well, as are the circumstances now. For a few days past it has not been quite so pleasant on account of the cold. Still, we have not suffered, as wood was plenty. Today is quite moderate. The health of the company continues good. I was rather surprised to hear of the death of George Forsyth.[1] This is, indeed, another singular circumstance. It seems that most of the deaths that occur among people of this age, that is, the male portion, are by accident of some kind. Oh, little can we tell the moment we may be called to go or to attend the last tribute paid to the remains of some departed friend. Thus, it is with life. Every evolution the Earth makes, thousands of human beings are rolled into the mighty gulf of eternity while we are all drawn one day nearer to the verge, and as time flies on we too will, at length, have accomplished our mission here and have passed away to make room for the coming throng. I will not say more on this subject now for my time is limited.

    I hope this will find you all well. It would please you to look into my nice little house which I have got papered with newspapers, with here and there a picture which, indeed, gives it quite a homely appearance.

    You will not have to send me the *Owego Times* as I have subscribed and will have it sent from the office.

    I must now bid you good night hoping to hear from you soon. I remain your affectionate son.

                                    Thomas

17.
                                    Camp of Detachment
                                    50th New York Volunteer Engineers
                                    Rappahannock Station, Virginia
                                    March 1st, 1864

Dear Father and Friends at Home,

    I was a little surprised the other day at opening an envelope and finding therein a comb, some thread, needles, pins, photographs, all of which come very acceptable to me. Indeed, I thank you for your kindness.
    I will send Alice some photographs in every letter as I now have some on hand for her album.
    There is little going on now. All still with us though I hear that a portion of the Army is in motion, but as yet am unable to tell what they have accomplished.
    This morning we arose and found the rain falling, and it has continued to do so all day, which makes it a little inconvenient for us. Still, I feel thankful that we are so well off. I am looking for a letter from home every day. I hope you are all well, at least as well, as this leaves me.
    I really believe if I had stayed home till now I would have been sick. I feel much better here and am somewhat fleshier than when at home. Still, I believe if the war was to end I would come home and try the climate again. Perhaps, if I did not have so much on hand it would agree with me better. The health of the company is fine. We expect some recruits soon. If they come, enough of them to fill the company, I am alright.[1] I presume Henry LaGrange is in Owego. Please let me know all the news. This is all now.
    My respects to all. I remain, your affectionate son,

                                    Thomas J. Owen
                                    Orderly, Company I
                                    50th New York Volunteer Engineers
                                    Washington

18.
                    Camp of Detachment
                    50th New York Volunteer Engineers
                    Rappahannock Station, Virginia
                    March 5th, 1864

Dear Father and Friends at Home,

    Your kind letter of the 1st came to my possession yesterday. There is little going on now with us. We received ten recruits Thursday. Lester Champlin[1] was among them, also Fred Hunt.[2] I am afraid we will not fill the company up. It seems that most of the men that have been enlisted for the company have been coaxed away.[3] We have now 109 men in the company. The health of the company is very good. We are having fine times, and fine weather. I am engaged two hours each day drilling the recruits.

    I wish you or Alice would get me another ½ dozen photographs from Berry[4] and send them to me. I will send two in this for Alice's album (Jeff Ferguson[5] and A.B. Beers[6]). Let me know if you get them.

    It is hard to form any idea of what will be done this spring. I do not believe this army will do much hard fighting. Still, we cannot tell. There has been some little stir of late but I am not able to say what it has amounted to. I will now bid you good night. I hope to hear from Alice soon.

                    Yours,

                    Thomas

19.
                            Camp of Detachment
                            50th New York Volunteer Engineers
                            Rappahannock Station, Virginia
                            February 20th, 1864

Dear Father, Sister Alice, and Friends at Home,

    It is with feelings of pleasure that I seat myself this evening to pen a few lines to you in answer to yours of the 7th which came to hand the 10th.

    Well, we are still here and things go on about the same. Yesterday we received eleven new recruits. The company now contains 120 men, thirty more, and then. None of this last lot are from our place. Four are from Susquehanna County, the other seven from Albany. We feel confident that the company will be filled up. Today has been very pleasant though a little muddy caused by the rain that fell yesterday and day before. I was much pleased today at receiving a letter from Milicent.[1] She is well, etc.

    We keep pretty busy now fixing up new tents for the recruits which are here and those we expect along soon. I have now 102 men here, the other 18 are on detached service in Washington. As a general thing, the company is healthy. I never enjoyed better health.

    We have no idea of a move; still, we are liable to go at any moment. It cannot be long. At the longest, ere the spring campaign opens, and for my part, if we are going to settle up this summer, the sooner we get at it the better. Oh, how I long to see the end of this struggle. How I long to again return to civil life and enjoy the blessings of peace which, to me, will be all the sweeter for having participated in the strife. I sometimes think of what I will go at when the war is over, but as yet have come to no conclusions. I rather think I will be to[o] lazy to work much; however, I will not make calculations to[o] far ahead.So, I will let matters run and be governed by circumstances when the death knell of the <u>rebellion</u> shall echo from state to state throughout this grand and <u>glorious Republic</u>, and let us hope that ever after, each and every sister <u>state will lend</u> a will[ing] hand to assist in keeping aloft our noble motto, <u>E pluribus unum.</u>

    I send in this two pictures of a scene near Yorktown, Virginia. One is No. 1 Battery, the other No. 4 Battery.[2] I have often been to both these places; in fact, we helped build the same. I could tell you a good deal about these pictures if I had time. You see that large [gun?] in No. 4?[3] Well, I have stood near that and at the same time heard the shells go whistling overhead, fired from the rebels in Yorktown, but I will not say more now. I hope you will find a place for them in you album or somewhere else so I

can see them if I get back.
This is all this time, goodnight,

Thomas

Battery No. 1, near Yorktown, Virginia, May 1862. *Photograph Collection, Engineer Historical Division.*

20.

Rappahannock Station, Virginia
March 18th, 1864

Dear Father, Sister, and Friends at Home,

    I now have a little spare time which I think cannot be spent to better advantage than in penning a few lines to you.

    Yours of the 14th came to hand this P.M. and is now before me. I am pleased to hear that you are well. We are having a little more to do of late than [is?] common, such as drilling. Squad drill from 8 to 9 A.M., company drill from 10 to 11½, battalion drill from 1½ to 3½ P.M., dress parade at 4 P.M., guard mounting at 4½. So you see the greater part of the day is occupied.

    There is a little a stir about camp concerning the <u>rebs</u>. Report says that two brigades of them have crossed the river below and threaten an attack,[1] which, I think will not be for their interest to do, as we have made some preparations for them and intend to give them a real Yankee welcome. We have two pieces of artillery planted in camp, and the latter we have surrounded with a brush barricade. The orders tonight are for every man to be ready to fall in at a moment's notice. Still I do not apprehend much danger, but it is well to be on the safe side and be ready.

    The captain tells me that there is no doubt about the company being filled up. Everything goes of[f] finely. Some of the boys have mumps and measles. As yet, little is said about General Grant's[2] taking command of this department. We all expect to know him better before long. I think something will be done soon. Everything seems to look like work, and I sincerely hope U.S.[3] will do as well here as he has done [in the?] <u>West</u>. With respect to all, I remain,

                      Yours,

                      Thomas J. Owen

21.
                      Camp Detachment
                      50th New York Volunteer Engineers
                      Rappahannock Station, Virginia
                      April 14th, 1864

Dear Father,

    I send you twenty dollars this morning. You may expect more soon. For reasons I will not now mention, I retain the rest of my pay for a few days.
    I am quite [well].

                      Your affectionate son,

                      Thomas

22.
                    Camp Detachment
                    50th New York Volunteer Engineers
                    Rappahannock Station, Virginia
                    April 16th, 1864

Dear Father,

    Thinking a line from me welcome anytime, I will occupy your attention a few moments this evening. You remember when I sent my check a day or two since, that I told you I would keep the rest of my pay for reasons I then would not mention. Well, I can now tell you the reason.

    By today's mail I received a commission as Second Lieutenant of Engineers in the 50th New York Volunteers from Governor Seymour of New York, dating from the 17th of March.[1] Father, I now hope to be able to help you more than ever. Of course, it will cost me something for my new outfit. I must have a horse and equipments and many other things an officer cannot get along without.

    I know you will be pleased to know that I have conducted myself so as to gain the confidence of my captain and colonel, who have been kind enough to recommend me for this position, and I hope I may prove worthy of the trust they have so kindly bestowed on me.

    My health is good. The weather is very changeable, some rain today. Two men of our company have died lately of fever, namely William H. Kipp[2] of Union and Aaron Fridley[3] of Seneca Falls, New York. We sent both home. Quite a number of the men are ailing. Water is bad that we use. Think the sooner we move the better for us.

    I must now close hoping this finds you all well. I remain yours with great respect,

                    Lieutenant Thomas J. Owen
                    Company I
                    50th New York Volunteer Engineers

Colonel William H. Pettes, Commander, Fiftieth New York Volunteer Engineer Regiment. *National Archives photograph 111-B-5593.*

23.   Camp 50th, New York Volunteer Engineers
Rappahannock Station, Virginia
April 23d, 1864

Dear Father,

Your kind note of the 19th came by today's mail. I am indeed much pleased to hear from you. Likewise to know the money I sent has reached its destination.

Well, we are making preparations for the coming contest, which at the longest cannot be postponed much longer. Some of the detachments have joined their respective corps. Company I is building a stockade at Warrenton Junction which shows that this line of communication is to [be] kept. Captain Folwell, with part of the company, has been there two days, and in the morning, the rest of the company goes there to help complete the work. I am going and will take command while the captain is absent, as he has other matters to attend to here about the trains, etc. Lieutenant Folwell[1] is going to work on the payrolls. We all have something to do.

I now live with Captain and Lieutenant Folwells who, by the way, [are] fine men and good officers. I like them much. I have not yet succeeded in getting a horse but have a clue of one. I was assigned to duty as lieutenant on the 19th by Colonel Pettes.[2] Things go well. For two or three days I have not felt well. Yesterday, I had quite a fever but today I feel much better, no fever. The headquarters of the regiment goes back to Washington in the morning, that is, Colonel Pettes, etc., leaving Lieutenant Colonel Spaulding in command of the pontoniering of the Army of the Potomac.

Hoping this finds you well, I am your most dutiful son,

Lieutenant T.J. Owen

P.S. I received a letter from Milicent this P.M. She is well. Talke[d] of going to New York on business.

Thomas

Officers' quarters, Fiftieth New York Volunteer Engineer Regiment, Rappahannock Station, Virginia, March 1864. *Library of Congress photograph B8171-7604*

24.   Camp at Rappahannock Station
                                 April 30th, 1864

Dear Father and Friends at Home,

Without doubt you are looking for a letter from me ere this. I hope you will pardon me for not writing before. I now acknowledge the receipt of two letters dated March 20th and 27th. I know not why I have this delayed unless it is because I have had more on hand to do of late than usual.

Since my last, I have been to Washington. Had a very fine time. Stayed in the city from the 24th until the 29th. I will, in haste, review my visit for your benefit, for I know you are somewhat anxious to know what I am about. Well, on the 22d March, Captain Folwell, Sergeant Bacon[1] and myself received orders to report to a court-martial convened in the city of Washington at the camp of the 15th New York Volunteer Engineers, which by the way is near the headquarters of the 50th. So, on the 24th we took the cars at Rappahannock Station at 9:45 A.M. and trundled along over the rough railroad to said city where we arrived at 2½ P.M. The case on trial was that of George Marshall[2] for desertion, he having deserted from Company I, 50th New York Volunteer Engineers about the 25th of January 1863. The order was for us to report on the morning of the 25th. After arriving in the city, we went up to camp where I saw quite a number of boys in Company M from Owego.

The captain stopped in camp but Sergeant Bacon and myself chose to stop outside of camp. So, we went downtown and took rooms at the Casparis Hotel,[3] which by the way is a quiet, respectable boarding house situated near the Capitol and patronized by several Congressmen who make it their home during their sojourn in the capital. Well, on the morning of the 25th (Friday) we reported to the court. Told us to come the next day as they could only take the testimony of the captain then. So we, Bacon and myself, went back to our boarding place and during the rem[ainder] of the day amused ourselves about the city. I went into the Capitol and examined Rogers' bronze door.[4] I will send you a history of the same which will be interesting if you have not read it. On Sunday I attended church at the Episcopal Church on 3d Street.[5] The discourse was handled well and was very appropriate for the day, "The Resurrection of our Savior." On Monday we again reported, and I was dismissed without having given my testimony, which was nothing more than what the captain testified to. On Tuesday, I returned to my company which I found full, complete to 150 men. Thus you see, I have quite a company to look after. Still, things go very well. My health is very good.

There has [sic] been some changes in the company. What

were Corporals Pierce,[6] O.L. Newell,[7] Bodle,[8] [and] Surdam,[9] are Sergeants. J. Perkins,[10] Probasco,[11] C. LaGrange,[12] J.H. Bunzey, and some others are corporals.

The headquarters with the regiment joined us on Wednesday last, the 30th. There are ten companies here now. Company A is in Washington and E is at Hazel Run,[13] making twelve in all, all of which are full except two, and they nearly. We have just had quite a cold storm which is rather hard on Company M and others that came from Washington and have not had time to build quarters.

I will close, promising to write again soon.

I remain your dutiful son,

      Thomas
      Orderly [sic], Company I

25.

Camp of Detachment
near Zoan Church[1]
4 Miles from Fredericksburg
May 14th, 1864

Dear Father and Friends at Home,

I embrace this, my first opportunity, of communicating with you since this long and severe fight commenced.

Had I the time I would be glad to go back and give you the full details of our doings since the 29th of April, but I have not, suffice to say. I have been in the saddle a good part of the time both night and day. We bridged the Rappahannock at Kelly's Ford with our flying train on the 29th for Gregg's [2] Cavalry to cross on. Took it up morning of 30th and went on toward the Rapidan.

On the 4th May, bridged the Rapidan at Ely's Ford at daylight. Took up bridge at ten o'clock (after a good portion of the 2d Corps[3] having crossed) and went on. Stayed the night at Chancellorsville. The 5th, the fight began. We went nearly to the front on the left with our train but came back faster than went, to Chancellorsville where we left the train and went the same night with arms and ammunition to the front. Reported to General Warren,[4] Commanding 2d Corps.

On the morning of the 6th at daylight, we went into the line of battle, front of the old Wilderness Tavern,[5] where we remained twenty-four hours in rifle pits back of the first line of battle. There were no casualties in Company I. One man of Company E was hit with a piece of shell in the head, did not kill him.[6] The fighting raged in front of us all day. We had a good position which we made better during the day by throwing up rifle pits, etc.

The 7th, we came out of the pits at daylight and lay at General Warren's headquarters all day. At night, returned to Chancellorsville. The 8th, went out toward Spotsylvania Court House. Came back. Then went over the Ny River and camped on the eve of the 10th, when we came back to the plank road and camped on Bensen's Farm[7] until the eve of the 12th, when we came to this place, taking all night for it.

We received General Orders from General Meade stating that we had taken 8,000 prisoners, 22 stands colors, 18 pieces artillery.

I hope this will reach you for I know you are anxious. I am well. The Army is now getting supplies from Belle Plain.

The wounded are in Fredericksburg. In your last, you did not know that 2d lieutenants had to have a horse. Let me say that all commissioned of the Engineer Corps have to be mounted. It is the highest branch of service. The pay is better and their duty requires them to be mounted.[8] I have a horse.

Ponton bridge across river in Virginia, 1864. *Library of Congress photograph B8171-748.*

Oh, I am anxious to hear from you. My respects to all.

I remain yours truly,
Lieutenant T.J. Owen

[For additional information relating to incidents and experiences that Owen describes in letters 24 and 25, please see the diary near the end of this publication.]

26.
                      Camp of Detachment
                      50th New York Volunteer Engineers
                      On the south bank of the Pamunkey
                      15 miles from Richmond
                      May 30th, 1864

Dear Father and Friends at Home,

    I am now sitting in my tent, which is pitched on the bank of the river neath the shade of a noble old maple. The sun is just setting and as I have a few moments' leisure, I will try and drop you a few lines. While I write, a heavy fight is going on between here and Richmond. Every instant I can hear the boom of the artillery knocking at the gates of the doomed city.

    This morning I received your two letters of the 15th and 21st. As you must know, there is [sic] no regular mails to or from the Army, so it is only once in a while that we get a letter or send one and even if there were, we have scarcely any time to write. For the last month we have been on the move nearly all the while, and as you very likely wish to know all about things, let me take you back to where we last parted, which was near Zoan Church, I believe.

    Just as I had finished my letter of the 14th, orders came to move, which we did and stopped again after going two or three miles, near Salem Church, where we stayed until the morning of 15th, then moved to Fredericksburg and camped just back of the city. This gave me a good chance to view the rebels' works on the heights, and I now wonder why any general would think of trying to take them from the river; but I cannot stay on the heights long for I have more important places to take you. The city was full of wounded which were being taken care of. The Sanitary Commission[1] was doing a noble work. The 16th, we lay in camp. The 17th, we broke camp at 5 A.M. and moved to Army headquarters at the front near Spotsylvania Court House.

    Camped near the Ny River. On the morning of the 18th, we broke camp and moved two miles to the right, when the train was ordered back to former camp. I stay[ed] until noon with the company, building a corduroy bridge, and then went back.

    The 19th, we lay quiet in camp until 5 P.M. when the enemy made a desperate attack on our right wing but were handsomely checked by the heavy artillery acting as infantry. This was their first flight, they having just come from the fortifications of Washington. The 20th was spent in camp until about dusk, when the company received orders to move, and soon we were on our way with the 2d Corps. We passed the Fredericksburg and Richmond Railroad[2] four time[s]. Passed through Bowling Green, about

Ponton wagon and wooden ponton, Fiftieth New York Volunteer Engineer Regiment, Rappahannock Station, Virginia, March 1864. *Library of Congress photograph B8184-7160.*

Canvas ponton, Fiftieth New York Volunteer Engineer Regiment, Rappahannock Station, Virginia, March 1864. *Library of Congress photograph B8171-7273.*

noon, the 21st, which is one of the finest little places I have seen. Crossed the Mattaponi at Milford and went into camp soon after. General Hancock[3] immediately began fortifying himself.

There was a slight skirmish here this morning between the 5th New York Cavalry[4] and a party of rebs who were trying to hold the station. The 5th took 72 prisoners. The 22d, Sunday, we lay quiet in camp, expecting an attack. 23d, broke camp early and moved south to the North Anna River. The morning of the 24th, we bridged that stream with two bridges just below the railroad bridge which was on fire at the same time. The enemy had just been driven over the river and when they left, the[y] set fire to the bridge.

The 25th, we laid another bridge above the railroad. On the morning of the 26th, we took up all of our bridges on the North Anna, they having been relieved by the wooden bridges. At noon we started for Chesterfield where we joined Sheridan's[5] cavalry and immediately went southeast down the Pamunkey which we struck at daylight near the remains of Hanovertown, having marched all night as fast as cavalry. This was the 27th. The enemy had a few skirmishers who were driven after firing a few shots. We immediately laid a bridge, and the cavalry went over. We remained there with the bridge until the night of the 27th, when Company I took what boats we had left after building the two bridges at Hanovertown and at midnight started for Huntley's Crossing,[6] several miles up the river, which we reached at daylight and laid our bridge. This was the main crossing. General Meade crossed at 9 A.M. and on the morning of the 29th, we took up the bridge and went back to Hanovertown. The morning of the 30th, we took up our bridge there and moved back to Huntley's Crossing, where we now lay in camp.

Time afternoon, 31st May, our bridge is on the wagons ready to move. There is a wooden ponton bridge here now. The weather is fine. Nearly every day since I last wrote there has been a hard battle fought. You must know nearly all the news. Yesterday, the 30th, there was a hard fight. I have not yet learned the particulars. Today the fighting is going on. It is southwest of us about 4 miles and about 12 from Richmond. I feel confident now of success. Communication is open from here to White House. The teams went today after rations, etc.

We have foraged some, it being necessary to do so in order to keep the teams and men in condition. This is a beautiful part of Virginia that we have just passed through. This being the first time the Army has ever been here, there is any quantity of stuff in the country, but we do not allow the men to pillage or take things. They ought not to. When we want anything, we send out a party, take it, and bring it to camp. The company, considering the hard work they have done, is in good condition, and we all feel as though we would sacrifice anything if it will only put down the rebellion.

We are now on the Peninsula[7] which, I believe as McClellan did, is the true way to Richmond. This month has been a bloody one, the most so, I think, of any during the war. The Army has done nobly. Lee[8] has been drawn and driven out of his favorite strongholds and now is in front of his darling city, but he has still more to do before he gets done with U.S.G.[9]

I hope to be able to tell you all about these movements before long when I shall have more time than I now have and when I can talk instead of write.

I have me a good boy for a servant. He was a house servant and is very handy. His name is Albert.[10]

Today I had a chance to send a letter, but as I had not time to finish this, I wrote an order for [you] to draw the interest on my money and send it. I hope soon to be able to relieve you if you need money. If you find it necessary, you can draw on the bonds in the bank, but I would rather send you the money if you can get along. Tell mother I am much better of[f] than I ever was before, since I have been in the Army. I now have a horse to ride, a servant to cook and look after my things, plenty of rations and good as we like or can get.

I must now come to a close. I was pleas[ed] to see that Alice has improved so much in writing. I hope she will stay in school by all means. Goodby[e] until next time.

> Your affectionate son and brother,
> Lieutenant Thomas J. Owen
> Company I
> 50th New York Volunteer Engineers

P.S. Evening, June 1st, we moved up to the front today. We are now 6 to 8 miles of Chickahominy. Hard fighting this P.M. Goodbye now,

> T.J. Owen

27.   Camp at Dunkirk,[1] Virginia
                                 June 20th, 1864

Dear Friends at Home,

   For the first time in a long while, I have a chance to pen you a few line[s]. (I send this by an officer who will mail it as soon as possible.)
   For the last fifteen days we have been with General Sheridan's Cavalry and every day during the time we have been on the march.
   On the 5th, the captain, myself, and 50 men of our company were ordered to the Cavalry Corps with a ponton train of eight boats. The 6th, we crossed the river Pamunkey at New Castle. We then proceeded northwest and on the 11th met the enemy near Trevilian Station, 9 miles east of Gordonsville. Fought all day and drove the enemy out. The 12th, moved up to the Station, fought all day, drove the enemy during the first part of the day but suffered a heavy loss. Took several hundred prisoners. On the night of the 12th, fell back very fast, having expended nearly all the ammunition, and the enemy having to[o] strong a force for us to withstand. We then came back passing through Spotsylvania Court House, Bowling Green, thence to King and Queen Court House where we lay on the night of the 18th. Yesterday, we came back to this place where we are now crossing the Mattaponi on the way, I expect, to White House. This has been a terrible raid. We took scarcely any rations or forage and have had to live on the country as we passed through.
   I am well as are the men. Have not heard from you in a long time. Can't tell when I shall write again. Goodbye,

                              Thomas J. Owen
                              Lieutenant, Company I
                              50th New York Volunteer Engineers

28.

Headquarters, Detachment
Engineers with Cavalry Corps
Debson's Landing[1]
James River
June 28th, 1864

Dear Friends at Home,

    We are now on the north bank of the James. Came here on the morning of the 25th and have been very busy helping cross the Cavalry Corps ever since. We brought with us from White House an immense wagon train, about 800 wagons in all. These all have to be ferried over in steamers and as the landing is not very good, it is slow work. The train will all be over today. We have not taken the pontons over yet as we have part of our bridge in use for a dock way.

    The move from White House took place on the night of the 22d or morning of the 23d. The eve of the 23d, we stopped at Wilcox's Landing, six miles above here, but were oblige[d] to pull out and came down here. The cavalry had a hard time of it, fighting to protect their train which the rebs seemed bound to have, but thanks to the good pluck of the Yankees they did not succeed.

    We will all be over the river in a day or two and I expect we will go back to General Grant's army. The weather is very warm, 103 below [sic] zero on the 27th in the shade. A fine shower yesterday towards night. Nice and cool today. I have had no mail this month except a let[ter] and by and by.

    I hope you do not worry about me for I am doing well. I feel somewhat anxious about you and hope to hear from you before long.

    I cannot tell when I will get [paid]. I have a little money with me and will send you some. Please give my respects to all. Your affectionate son,

    Thomas

29.   Camp of Detachment
        (Ponton Train No. 4)[1]
        50th New York Volunteer Engineers
        July 7th, 1864

Dear Father and Friends at Home,

  I confess I am now under obligation to you for two letters received on the 1st, dated respectively the 8th and 13th of June.

  I wrote you from White House about the 22d. Well, we did not make a very long stop at the above-mentioned place as you will soon see. On the morning of the 23d, long before the day had dawned, we were on our way to the James which we reached the same eve at 6 o'clock, having been detained on the way several hours by the enemy, who seemed to dispute our passage to the river. General Gregg with his division of cavalry fought well, and through his courage and skill, we succeeded in getting through. On the way, we passed through Charles City Court House. Arrived at the river. We went into camp expecting to stay all night, at least, but lo, about 9 o'clock, orders came to move immediately, and soon we were on the road, pontons ahead. From Wilcox's Landing, we went down the river to the neighborhood of Fort Powhatan,[2] which is situated on the south side of the river. We were on the road all night and just at daylight parked close to the river bank.

  Steamers were in waiting to ferry us over and soon the Cavalry Corps began crossing first by sending over their wagons, which took several days, there being about eight hundred of them. Though we were the first at the landing, we were the last to cross, being engaged in the meantime in loading the wagons and keeping the wharf in order, which kept us quite busy enough.

  On the morning of the 29th, everything being safely over, we loaded our train and crossed the noble James. Landed at Windmill Point,[3] where we went into camp for a short time.

  At 4 P.M., received marching orders and soon were on the way to City Point, the cavalry going at the same time off to the left of the Army to help General Wilson[4] (3d Division) out of trouble. The train arrived at this place early on the 30th. We joined our old detachment, which we easily found, and went into camp. Indeed, it seemed like getting home after having been on the march for nearly a month during which time we traveled several hundred miles in the heat and dust of Virginia.

  Since we have been here, we have had very little to do. On the 4th I went up to the front where I participated in a fine Fourth of July dinner given by the 1st Battalion, 50th New York Volunteer Engineers, commanded by Major Brainerd.[5] It was a fine affair and did honor to its <u>donors</u>. Since then, little has occurred worth notice save the continual boom boom of the artillery firing on Petersburg, which, by the [way], I had the pleasure of seeing on the 5th, that is, from a distance of several miles.

This afternoon the companies received orders to go to the front. Captain Folwell and Captain Van Brocklin[6] of Company C have both gone. I remain with about 30 men in charge of both trains and anticipate a fine time. Yours, with respects to all,

                Thomas

30.
       Headquarters, Detachment
       [Ponton Train] No. 4
       50th New York (Cavalry Corps)
       Light House Point[1]
       Virginia
       July 21st, 1864

Dear Friends at Home,

 Why I do not get any news from you I cannot tell, but I can tell the reason why you have not [heard] from me for the last few days.

 Our company is now attached to the Cavalry Corps and are [sic] stationed near headquarters of said corps, which is at Light House Point, on the James, 5 miles below City Point. We came here on the 12th, this month. Since then, we have been very busy repairing our train and, by the way, I have been appointed quartermaster for this detachment. This gives me plenty to [do] as I have no clerk yet. We have with us 42 wagons in all, which requires 252 mules to haul the same.

 There are 18 boats (canvas) in this train. We can bridge 400 feet. Now, I hope you do not expect [to] hear much war news from me. If so you are disappointed. Now and then we get a paper in which we see that we are yet in front of Petersburg (news ain't it) and I have no very definite idea how long we will stay here. I think I can stand it as we have a pretty camp and good quarters. As the mail is going soon, I will not have time to write anymore now. I am well, as is the company generally. Please give my respects to all who inquire.

       Your affectionate son,
       Lieutenant Thomas J. Owen
       Acting Assistant Quartermaster
       Ponton Train No. 4
       Cavalry Corps

31. 　　　　　　　　Camp of Detachment
　　　　　　　　　　50th New York Volunteer Engineers
　　　　　　　　　　near City Point, Virginia
　　　　　　　　　　August 10th, 1864

Dear Friends at Home,

　　I have forgotten almost but I believe there is one letter of yours that I have not answered, but it's of little account whether there is or not. I will write at least. On the 8th, we moved from Light House Point (where we have been laying for some time) to this place which is near City Point and almost in the same place we were before going down there. The captain and Lieutenant Folwell have gone to the front with part of the company. I remain with the train and the majority of the company to take care of it. Do not imagine for an instant that I have nothing to do, for that is not the case when the company joined the Cavalry Corps. I was appointed quartermaster of the detachment. Therefore you see why I am with the train. I must stay and take care of the property in my charge. There are 47 wagons in all and about 300 public animals—horses and mules—together with the accompanying appendages—[which] make quite enough for one man. I am now making out my papers for the month of July. I have a clerk but he has not learned the business yet so I am kept pretty close.

　　Yesterday, there was a terrible explosion at the Point. The immense pile of ammunition stored on the wharf blew up, completely demolishing everything near it. I believe it originated in a vessel load of the same then laying at the dock. I have not been able to learn the loss of life but it is estimated at 2 or 3 hundred, mostly colored, who were engaged in unloading supplies at the dock.[1] Fragments of bodies and materials about the building were blown several hundred yards from the spot. The general expression of all that have seen it is it's awful. There has [sic] been several deaths in the company since the 21st of July. We have lost four men, the first was George Dan[2] from Jacksonville; 2d, James Randall[3] from Vestal Broome; 3d, Squire A. Kimber[4] from Owego; the last was poor Charley Stratton[5] of Owego. He was a good soldier and one that we all miss. He was also one of the veterans and was home when I was, last winter. He is the first of the lost that reenlisted last winter to lay down his life on the altar of his country and may he be the last. We have sent him home. I presume ere this he has been interred by those who best know where to lay the remains of their friend and noble soldier. I am quite well. The company is doing very well now. I hope we will not lose any more. I think if they can stand it throug[h] August they will come out all right.

One particular pester here now is the flies. O[h], you cannot imagine how they act. The animals go almost frantic. They can take no peace during the day and we keep both hands in motion most of the time brushing them away. I never saw anything of the kind at home. I must now bid you good night. I hope you are all well. My respect to all.

                        I am very respectfully,
                        Your obedient son and brother,
                        Lieutenant Thomas J. Owen

32.

Headquarters
Ponton Train No. 4
near City Point, Virginia
August 24th, 1864

Dear Friends at Home,

It seems quite a long time since I have heard from you. If I mistake not, your last letter was dated July 19th, almost a month. I presume you have written and through somebody's carelessness I have not received them. However, we will let that drop. I will write about so often whether I get answers or not.

We are still laying quiet near City Point. Nothing of any importance has taken place here except that we have had some considerable rain which has in a measure rid us of our active and troublesome enemy, the fly. One that has not been here and seen for himself cannot imagine what a pester this little insect is.

Today, I was up to the front to see the captain but was disappointed as he was out with part of his men cutting a road on the left of our lines in the vicinity of the 5th Corps.[1] I was unable to learn anything definite except that the Weldon Railroad[2] is completely cut and that we are holding the position. This is pretty good and in time must tell on the enemy. There is a usual, almost continual, firing between the two armies, and I now have no doubt that General Grant will be successful in accomplishing his object. A good reinforcement is what we want here just now. Our noble army has been reduced a great deal during the campaign but what there is left is of the true stamp, and though we all want peace, we want a union more. Peace-and-the-Union, no botchwork about it. Now I do not like War. Neither do I like soldiering as a profession, but I do not feel as though I could even think of abandoning the cause until the Glorious Cause we have undertaken is successful. How I wish some of them at home could think so and come down here and help stop this bloody war, but I am afraid some will have to be drafted from our country before the call quota is filled. O[h], how I pity the poor wretches afraid to help maintain their Government. I believe I'd sooner be shot than scared to death.

I hope to hear from you soon. Please direct to the regiment as you used to, as I will get them sooner.

In good health, I remain,

Very respectfully,
Your obedient son,
Lieutenant Thomas J. Owen
Acting Assistant Quartermaster
50th New York Volunteer Engineers

P.S. Alice,
 Enclosed you find a photograph of Lieutenant [Henry] LaGrange for your album.

Thomas

33.

        Camp of Detachment
        50th New York Volunteer Engineers
        near City Point, Virginia
        August 28th, 1864

Dear Father and Friends at Home,

    I have been looking for the last few days for a letter from you and today it came bearing date August 13th, which shows it has been some time on the way. Why this delay and who to blame for it is entirely out of our knowledge. There seems to be something wrong. I have written you quite often as I always intend to do whenever it is practicable.
    It is a beautiful Sunday afternoon. Everything is quiet, "remarkably so." I do not even hear the heavy boom of the heavy guns in front of the doomed city.[1] We are still in our nice little camp near City Point. Everything goes on very nicely. My animals are now doing well. I have just 300. The flies are not as bad as they have been. The health of the men is, I think, a little better as a general thing. I hear from the part of the company with the captain quite often. They were in the rifle pits the other night and by the way that was the same night we had the scare here which was on the 25th of August. Now there are several ponton trains laying here in the neighborhood of each other. Otherwise, there is not much force just about. Well, on the afternoon of the day mentioned, Captain Personious[2] (of Company G and commander [of] the train laying next to me) came and showed me an order from headquarters ordering us to post a picket and to be ready to hitch up and take the trains to City Point in case of an attack which was anticipated might be made by the enemy's cavalry as several thousand of them [   ]. We in our lines . . . the picket was posted. Night came on and so did a heavy thunder shower which lasted about half the night. I had given orders to the guard to wake me in case he should hear any alarm or firing.
    Nothing except the wind and rain disturbed us until about 2½ A.M. when I plainly heard the report of several guns in the direction of the picket. The guard called out lustily but I was ahead of him. In a few moments the men were ready to repel the foe should he show himself but as we heard no more firing we concluded the picket had made a mistake or at least that the enemy was not upon us and accordingly allowed the men to again retire while I mounted my horse and rode out to see what the matter was. When I came to the post, I found them all alive and in line. It seems two or three horsemen had rode up and, being challenged by the sentinel, did not halt but fired on him. The sentinel returned the fire and the horsemen galloped off. The next morning the picket was

taken in and since then nothing has transpired to disturb the tranquility of the camp.

I am enjoying myself very well.
With kind regard to all.
I remain most respectively,
Your dutiful son,
Lieutenant Thomas J. Owen
50th New York Volunteer Engineers and Acting Assistant Quartermaster with Ponton Train No. 4

P.S. Alice. One photograph enclosed of James H. Perkins of this company.

Thomas

34.	Camp of Detachment
50th New York Volunteer Engineers
near City Point, Virginia
August 31st, 1864

Dear Father and Friends at Home,

    I acknowledge the receipt of yours of the 25th and feel much pleased to hear from you.

    Today was muster day so we now have six months' pay due us. When we will get it, I am unable to say, but I think it will not be long hence.

    Yesterday, I was up to the front and found the company had moved the day before out to the Weldon Railroad on the left with the 5th Corps. Wishing to see the captain, I went out there and found all hands at work on a fort just beyond the railroad. I was much pleased with the look of things and believe there is [sic] not rebs enough in the neighborhood of Petersburg to drive us out of this good position. The works are good and there is plenty of them but I shall know more about them in a few days and then I will tell you more particularly. This afternoon I received the following ~~order~~ note which I will copy:

    Headquarters, Detachment
50th New York Volunteer Engineers
in front of Petersburg, Virginia
August 31st, 1864

Lieutenant

    We have so much work for our officers on the various works in front of Petersburg that I am obliged to gather them in for this duty wherever I can get them. I therefore send you the enclosed order not from any dissatisfaction with the manner in which you have performed your duties as acting assistant quartermaster, but as a matter of necessity.

    Respectfully,
I. Spaulding, Lieutenant Colonel
Commanding

Lieutenant Thomas J. Owen
Acting Assistant Quartermaster
Ponton Train No. 4

    Well, the order was for me to turn over all quartermaster property in my possession to Lieutenant McNaught,[1] quartermaster of the reserve battalion, which I will do in the morning and then, as soon as I can make up my papers for the month, I shall join the company for duty which will be in a few days. The reason of this is there is no pontoniering to do now and it is not likely there will be any for some time to come. The principal work is on the fortifications as you see by the colonel's note. The weather is fine. Now and then a little shower. The flies are quite civil though not quite so much so as we could wish. Everything goes well. I am enjoying good health and am quite well pleased with the duties of quartermaster but that is my nature. I always try to make myself contented and try to be pleased with anything that it is my duty to be engaged in. As you say, I hope this bloody war will be brought to a close ere long, but yes, that's if there is something besides peace that we want more and that is what we are all fighting for. I hope this will find you all well.

                         With my respects to all,
                         I remain your affectionate son and brother
                         Lieutenant Thomas J. Owen
                         Company I
                         50th New York Volunteer Engineers

P.S. I see Alice has not written in the last two letters. What's the matter? I am always pleased to hear from her.

                                    Thomas

35.   Camp of Detachment
                       50th New York Volunteer Engineers
                       near City Point, Virginia
                       September 15th, 1864

Dear Father and Friends at Home,

    Yours of the 5th and 6th came to hand the 12th. I am indeed happy to hear that our beautiful town is free from the "draft."
    I am much pleased to see the new troops coming in. This looks as though the people of the North were still alive and anxious to close this terrible war. It is now understood here that the Army of the Potomac is as strong as when it crossed the Rapidan. This is encouraging to us. The only thing now to hinder a speedy "peace" is the difference of opin[ion] at the North. I believe the Army is all right in reference to the coming election and feel confident that Mr. "Lincoln" will receive the support of the soldiers now in the field, all of whom well know the only true road to "peace."
    Yesterday, I went up to the headquarters of the 5th Army Corps on the Weldon Railroad. Captain Folwell is still engaged in that vicinity, fortifying, and I think if General Lee could see these works he would bid goodbye to any hopes, if he has any, of ever taking this line. Not only is the fortifying going on briskly, but extensive preparations are being made for the bad weather that will ere long set in. Miles of road are being covered with corduroy. A railroad has been constructed branching from the City Point and Petersburg Road to the Weldon Road[1] at 5th Corps Headquarters, so that now the cars run from City Point clear through to the left of the Army, passing right through the Army. It will be very convenient by and by when the roads become muddy as supplies will only have to be hauled a few miles at the farthest.
    But I am in hopes we will not lay here this winter. Every day now tells on the Rebellion and brings us reinforcements. General Lee will without doubt try to do something before long, but the monster (rebellion) is doomed. A few more struggles and he will fall prostrate before the loyal of the land, so let us cheer up and stand firm a short time longer and we will gain the rich reward for the many noble men of our land that have given their lives that the Nation might be preserved. When I think of all this, I cannot see how some men at the North think of having peace without first silencing this rebel gang. Talk about "compromising," indeed, and at this time of day to[o]. If a compromise was needed, why not have made it at first and saved the many noble hearts that have oozed out their life blood on southern soil, saved us from national debt and everything accompanying such a terrible war.

But the "People of the United States" said No, that these rebels had risen up against the Government and must be vanquished. Accordingly, we set about it and now, when we have them nearly subdued, there are "black-hearted" traitors in the northern states encouraging the enemy by talking about "peace at any price," "compromise," and the defect of the "Administration," all of which go in the balance on the side of the enemy, and I believe that this war would have been ended ere this had it not been for this class of men. No, that is to[o] good a name. What shall I call them? Traitors. No they are not as honorable as an outright traitor. Ah, I hav[e] it. Copperheads. That's it, and if you want to see any of their poisonous venom, look at the Chicago Pill[2] they fix up for General McClellan, but it turned his stomach and he could not swallow it. Think they had better "sugarcoat it" a little.

Now I am not particularly against General McClellan but I am against the party that has nominated him. I am against anyone who is not for the "Administration" and the prosecution of the war until we can have peace and a Union with it. One that will stand wherein there will be no slavery to again overthrow a peaceful and happy people, and I believe that is not far distant. I will now close. I think you know my mind on the war question now. Expecting to hear from you soon, I remain,

> Very respectfully,
> Your obedient son
> Lieutenant Thomas J. Owen
> 50th New York Volunteer Engineers
> and Acting Assistant Quartermaster
> Ponton Train No. 4

36.
Camp of Detachment
50th New York Volunteer Engineers
near City Point, Virginia
October 9th, 1864

Dear Father and Friends at Home,

It has been some little time since I have written you. Since I last wrote, we have been paid. I received 4 months' pay where 6 months were due me. I had been in hopes to send you a hundred or to [two?] dollars but living is so high, and not receiving all the pay due me, I find I have not much to spare. So, I will give you an order on Mr. Warner[1] for a couple of $50 bonds and you can get them cashed without trouble. I hope you will not fail to take them and use them if you are in as [   ] I know you must be. You have no idea how much this has troubled me of late. I knew you were looking for money from me and when you see none come, you must be disappointed.

I think, bye and bye, I can send some money home but I cannot now. I have things so that I shall not have to be laying out so much hereafter. I have also quit the use of tobacco entirely. This I did on the 1st of October. Cigars have become so high that I made up my mind to stop smoking and save 10 or 15 dollars a month. I am still acting assistant quartermaster with the train. Last Sunday we moved out to the front and back the same night. Not a very pleasant time as I was not feeling any to[o] well, in fact, have not been right well for some little time. On the 6th, I had a chill and another on the 8th, light touch of fever and ague, but I think I can drive it of[f] and come out all right. I have no news from the Army, only we are fortifying the advanced position on the left. Our regiment is now beyond the Weldon Railroad busy at that business. The weather is getting somewhat chilly and I begin seriously to think of building a fireplace. I hope you will write soon. I remain,

Truly, your obedient son,
Lieutenant Thomas J. Owen
50th New York Volunteer Engineers

37.   Camp of Detachment
                                  50th New York Volunteer Engineers
                                  near City Point, Virginia
                                  October 22d, 1864

Dear Father and Friends at Home,

    It was with feelings of joy that I read your kind letter of the 9th. The very kind line and the earnest sympathy shown in your invitation for me to come home all go to make my heart glad. I am very glad, indeed, that you received the order for the bonds and hope you had no trouble in getting them cashed. My health has improved and, as I told you before, what I meant to do, I think I have accomplished. That is, I have got rid of the fever and ague and glad am I to be able to say it for I tell you it is not a pleasant thing to have on hand (in fact, I think it most to[o] shaky). Yes, I am well again and able to fly about and see to things but about the furlough, not now. I shall try and come home this winter but don't look for me until you see me as I am utterly unable to say for certain when or whether I can come. The captain and Lieutenant Bain,[1] his brother, are both home now on twenty-day leave. We had what we call election[s] on the 20th, that is, the men were sworn and the ballots given them, one of each kind to every man, and he put which one he liked in the envelope and sent them to a voter of his town.[2] I sent mine to you and you know what kind of ticket it contains. As well as I can tell you, this is the first time I ever voted for President and I believe with my whole soul that I voted for the good of the country. May God grant that it may so turn out.

    O[h], we have glorious news from the valley again. Sheridan can crow ~~again~~ now. Things look about the same here with the exception that there is more earth on the top of the ground than there was, but I expect we will have to move soon now, for I have just been having my house fixed comfortable for the chilly weather that is coming on. I have a fine fireplace built and even now I sit here by my desk and write with a nice fire blazing away, which makes it almost as pleasant as home. No, I will not say that, though the fire burns just as bright and the room may be just as warm and comfortable. Still, there's no place like home. You may think that I have been away so long that I have become weaned from the place of my youth. To be sure, I do not feel homesick but I have a strong desire for this war to end that I may again enjoy the blessing of a civil life and the comforts of home.

    Not long since you spoke of a box for J.H. Perkins (poor fellow). Well, it came and as Lester Champlin was not here, I sold the contents and the money I send to his father. I cannot help feeling sad when I think of that noble boy. O[h], he was a fine soldier. None more ready and willing than he ever was to do his duty. Kind and obliging to his comrades as well as mannerly and soldierly in his bearing. Thus he won the respect of and goodwill of both officers and men of his company and regiment, but alas, he cut off in the springtime of life like many other noble youths of our land who have perished during this desperate struggle. Oh, may their dying groans ever haunt the traitors that have caused all this and those that would today prolong it an hour. Yea, may the bleeding skeletons of the many heroes that now lay bleaching on southern soil ever appear to them both day and night so that death to traitors will be a welcome guest. Yea, may the entering of the dark and bottomless pit be a relief. I will now close. Hope you will write soon and tell me all the news.

    I remain,

                      most respectfully,
                      Your obedient son,
                      Lieutenant Thomas J. Owen

38.   Camp near City Point, Virginia
                                     November 13th, 1864

Dear Father and Friends at Home,

Sunday morning. The sun shines bright and clear. I am feeling quite well and pen these few lines while my mail carrier is saddling his horse. We have the glorious news that Mr. Lincoln is again to steer the good old ship of State, thank God. I verily believe that the country is now comparatively safe and that before we vote for a national head again this horrid war will be ended, and those that are fortunate enough to go through can return home and again live a peaceful and happy life. "Oh," I often think how will it seem. Yesterday, I was up to see the captain again. He is feeling finely as are the men. There is little news. O[h], yes, Company M has rather bad luck with her officers, two of them having been lately dismissed the service of the U.S. The first was Lieutenant Waldo[1] for drunkenness while on duty. The other [was] Lieutenant Austin,[2] for disobedience of the 5th Article of War which forbids any officer or enlisted man using any disrespectful "language" towards the President, Vice President, Congress, or Chief Magistrate, or legislature of any of the United States, etc. Well, he is found guilty of this. Also, for conduct prejudicial to good order and military disciplin[e]. I expect he will be home soon but they can't send me home in that way ("rather come in a box"). The fact is I wouldn't come. I wish you all a pleasant good morning. Time is up. The hors[e] is saddled.

                                     Your most obedient son,
                                     Thomas

Alice, send a paper with a needle and thread in it. Black, if you please.

                                     Thomas

39.
                Camp of Detachment
                50th New York Volunteer Engineers
                near City Point, Virginia
                November 17th, 1864

Dear Friends at Home,

    Your very kind and welcome letter of the 10th came yesterday as did the messenger with the primer in it. Many thanks for your promptness. The boy will soon learn to read. He knows the letters now.

    Still, the glorious news of "election" keeps coming better and better, "thank God." The Union that has long withstood the thumping and banging of those cursed traitors that would bear it twain is today stronger than when they first began, but we are not only binding it together stronger and stronger, but we are polishing the old surface. Scouring off the old "black" "rusty" "spots" that came nigh, being its destruction, and soon it will shine forth "brighter" than ever, on a foundation the "world" cannot move. When I think of this, the cruel deeds of war, the fatigues, privations, and all seem to lose their horror and seem as but a shadow that will be seen but a short time in the bright surface of the glorious future, but their deeds will remain a shining light to the world, "ever proclaiming" "The people of the United States are able to sustain a government." A beacon light to the poor, "persecuted," and downtrodden, kindly inviting him to seek shelter and comfort beneath its "glowing rays."

    There is little news just now. We still remain quiet at City Point. Two men, recruits, have died lately. C. Crawford[1] joined the company last spring and C. Hollenbeick,[2] a new recruit, came this fall. Both bodies are to be sent to their friends. The men with me are quite healthy. The fever and ague is not so prevalent as it was. I have a shake now and then but think I will be all right soon. I received a letter from Milicent a day or two since. She inquires about Father and Alice and says she has not heard from them in some time. She is now in Green Point (near New York City). With my best wishes to all, I kindly bid you good morning.

                          Your Most Obedient Son,
                          Thomas

40.
                      Camp of Detachment
                      50th New York Volunteer Engineers
                      near Fort Stevenson,[1] Virginia
                      November 27th, 1864

Dear Father and Friends at Home,

    Yours of 20th came last eve. Since I last wrote we have moved from City Point to this place which is near Army headquarters about 1½ miles from the Weldon Railroad. Came here last week, Saturday the 19th, after having a very disagreeable march all night. To make it interesting for the traveler, the rain commenced falling just about the time we left camp and continued until Monday night. This made things a little unpleasant, and I must say we had the hardest time and suffered the most of anytime since the present campaign. However, I will not stop to describe the dark side of things. Suffice to say we are now quite comfortably situated in new quarters.

    When we moved up, there was a contemplated move of the Army which would doubtless have taken place had the weather remained fine. Still, it is not altogether abandoned but depends altogether on the weather.

    I was pleased a few days since on opening an envelope and finding not a letter but something that was almost as acceptable. That was thread, needles, and pins. Thanks for them all. The primer came. Likewise those other papers. The contraband[2] can say his letters and read a little. I shall learn him to spell "Alice" next. He learns easy but has many sly tricks. He likes sugar and, if not watched, will put a dozen or more spoonfuls in a little coffee or tea and many other little tricks, some of which are amusing, but I hope by perseverance to make him useful not only as a servant to me now but to his poor ignorant race, by and by, and may God speed the time when they all will be free to learn, if they choose, and elevate themselves from the low degraded state of the "slave."

    I spoke some time since about a box. If you send one, pleas[e] put in it four tea cups and saucers. Mother will do this, I know. I have been thinking some of coming home for a few days in January but cannot say with any certainty. Do not take it for granted that I will come, for it is very uncertain, and I do not wish you to be disappointed. Am feeling pretty well. I remain, dear parents, your affectionate son,

>Lieutenant Thomas J. Owen
>Company I
>50th New York Volunteer Engineers
>and Acting Assistant Quartermaster

[Written on margin] I am unable to say what became of James Perkins' watch, pen, and case but will make inquiry about it.

>Thomas

41.
                              Camp of Detachment
                              50th New York Volunteer Engineers
                              near Poplar Grove Church,[1] Virginia
                              December 6th, 1864

Dear Friends at Home,

    You see by the heading that we have again moved camp. We are now with the regiment near the yellow house.[2] Came here the 1st. Had a pleasant day to move and consequently a very pleasant move. The colonel has been very active fixing up for winter. He built houses for the quartermasters that all we had to do was to move in. We have a beautiful camp. Nothing about here compares with it. The weather is delightful but think it cannot last thus. Your letter of the 27th came the other day. I am glad you asked for the money, if you want it. Money was made to use. I send you the order enclosed. I also send for fifty for myself which I wish you to send to me immediately. I think it will come safe by mail. We will not get pay until sometime in January, and I do not wish to be without money. I am now entirely out. Whether I come home or not I am unable yet to say, but shall try after we get pay.
    I have not time now to say much. Please write soon.

                              I remain ever yours,
                              Lieutenant Thomas J. Owen
                              50th New York Volunteer Engineers
                              and Acting Assistant Quartermaster
                              4th Battalion, 50th New York

42.

Headquarters, Detachment
50th New York Volunteer Engineers
near Poplar Grove Church, Virginia
December 10th, 1864

Dear Father, Mother, and Sister,

    I hope you are all within hearing for I have communications from each of you to answer and I hope none of you will chide me for writing you all at the same time as I always intended to do. Father and Alice's letter came a day or two since, dated the 3d. It always makes my heart leap with joy to hear from any of you, that you are well, etc., and Alice please do not think I mean to flatter you when I say your letter was excellent. There is only one fault I have to mention and that is I came to the end to[o] soon. Let me say there is no necessity for your saying, as you sometimes do, that you think I must be getting tired of your nonsense, etc., for I assure you I will not, so that is no longer an excuse. Mother's letter of the 5th came last evening and it is useless for me to say I was much pleased and I hope she will always say something when any of you write.

    Just now there is quite a stir among us. A few days since, one canvas train was sent with the 5th Corps. Where they have gone or what has been accomplished I am unable to say. The other pontons have gone back to their old camps at City Point so that my train is the only one remaining here and I am quartermaster for headquarters. We have a fine camp. I have a good log house and feel quite at home. Yesterday, there was [sic] some prospects of a move. Last night the men were all ready, the teams hitched up until about 8 P.M. when we received orders to unhitch. This was carefully done. About the same time it commenced storming. A sort of sleet fell all night and this morning the ground was white with a light coating of wet snow. Yesterday was the coldest day of the season. Froze all day. Moderated during the night, and today is quite pleasant overhead.

    We hold ourselves in readiness to move, but I think it depends on the movements of the 5th Corps whether we go or not, at least move or no. I am not going to bother my brain speculating on possibilities. I think we will soon settle down for winter, and it would please me to stay where I am.

    I hope this finds you all feeling well and in as good nature as it leaves me. I am improving in health every day. The company is quite healthy, though I am not with it now. Still, I feel a deep interest in the noble boys with whom I have served so long. If people ask how I am, tell them to write and ask me after giving them my respects.

>I remain most respectfully,
>Your dutiful son and brother,
>Lieutenant Thomas J. Owen
>50th New York Volunteer Engineers
>and Acting Assistant Quartermaster
>4th Battalion
>Army of Potomac

43.

Headquarters, Detachment
50th New York Volunteer Engineers
near Poplar Grove Church, Virginia
December 16th, 1864

Dear Father, Mother, and Sister,

    Yours of the 11th came last evening (containing the receipt). I have some scruples about my ability to express the feelings of thankfulness that I feel towards you for this kind favor, and I hope to surprise you one of these days by returning a much larger amount.

    You remember in my last I had no thought that we were even then on the point of moving. Well, so it is in the Army. One cannot tell what the coming hour may bring to light. I had just deposited your letter in the box when the colonel notified me to have a portion of the train ready to move immediately. The whole command was ordered out and soon we were on the move. The lat[e] rain had made the roads somewhat muddy but things went off pretty well. Traveled all night and about daylight came to a halt near the bank of the Nottoway River, distant about 20 miles from camp. A portion of the 9th Corps[1] went with us. After taking some breakfast, we received orders to bridge the stream. This we did in a very short time, using eight boats. As soon as this was done the 5th Corps began crossing from the opposite side, they having been out tearing up the Weldon Railroad, etc. The Corps finished crossing just at dusk. We then took up the bridge and camped until 2 o'clock A.M. when we started back to camp where we arrived at noon the same day. The return was quite as unpleasant as the going out, though there was no mud, but the ground was frozen very hard. The wind was very bitter, indeed, making it impossible to keep warm riding. In fact, I think it was the most unpleasant day I ever saw in the service, but when we arrived in camp and found good fires blazing away in our good log tents, we soon forgot the cold. Since then, there has been no move with us. We are busy building, and the camp begins to look like a city. I sent to the [City] Point today and found the $50.00. It came much quicker than I expected and I thank you again for your promptness. My time is limited. I remain very truly, your obedient son and brother,

                  Thomas

44.
                         Headquarters, Detachment
                         50th New York Volunteer Engineers
                         near Poplar Grove Church, Virginia
                         January 6th, 1864

Dear Father, Mother, and Sister,

I had hoped to be able to let you know ere this when I could come home, but as yet it is uncertain.

We still remain in winter camp. Time passes quite pleasantly as we are very comfortably situated. Today, a man belonging to the 2d Corps was executed near our camp for desertion. I saw him shot. Every Friday, some poor victim has to pay the penalty of the law with his life. A week ago last Friday, I saw three hanged. Last Friday, one was hanged but I did not go to see him. Today there were two shot.[1] How many more will follow I cannot say. It looks hard to see a man in the prime of life thus cut off and in such a manner, for better had he feel [fell?] by the hands of the enemy, but if they will break the law they must suffer the consequences.

The weather has been quite cold this year until the last day or two. Today has been rainy and the mud is ankle deep.

There is little news about the Army. The pickets keep up the usual music. Our detachment is doing a little work on the fortifications. One company is building a tower[2] which is to be used by the Signal Corps. There is a report that another expedition has gone down the coast.[3] Hope it will meet with better success than the last.

I was thinking a little while ago where I was a year ago tonight. How well I remember it and how short the year seems. Why the very voice of Edward Kirk[4] seems [to] still ring in my ear, and I say to myself, can it be possible that it is a year ago tonight that I heard him, but when I look back and see the scroll of events that have happened, I am almost surprised to see so much accomplished in so short a space.

I have not heard from Milicent in some time.

Hoping this finds you all well.

I will kindly bid you all a hearty good night.

                         Your obedient son and loving brother,
                         Lieutenant Thomas J. Owen
                         50th New York Volunteer Engineers
                         and Acting Assistant Quartermaster

45.   Headquarters, Detachment
         50th New York Volunteer Engineers
         near Poplar Grove Church, Virginia
         January 22d, 1864

Dear Father, Mother, and Sister,

 Many thanks for your kind invitation to me in your last, dated the 15th January. Indeed I would gladly comply, but not yet. Wait a little longer. I saw the colonel tonight and he told me he though[t] I could go next month (February). Alice, you little witch, you almost made me uneasy telling about the sleighing and etc. I had thought to get away before this time but there were so many that did not go last winter that those that did have to stand back a little while. We can have 5 or 6 go at a time, and as some have just been, the colonel thinks we will all have a chance.

 The weather during the last week was beautiful up to yesterday, which was made very disagreeable by a rapid and continuous fall of rain which froze almost as fast as it fell. Today (Sunday) has been, I would say, pleasant were it not for the mud. By the way, we are building a church,[1] and as we have had preaching only twice this winter, hope that when it is done, we will be a little more human and have it every Sunday. We always try to regard the day by refraining from the daily work of the week. I have been reading most of the day, which I enjoy very much.

 I presume Alice has been to church and Sunday school if it was not to[o] cold. I was looking over some of my old Sunday school lessons today in the Testament and it seemed so fresh that I could hardly imagine it had been so long since I learned them.

 Everything goes nicely. The rebellion is crumbling away, and I must soon begin to think about some other business. Johnnies coming in every day. I see the <u>reb</u> papers say they did not care anything about Fort Fisher and Wilmington.[2] If that is so, why did they build the former and mount 72 guns in it to protect the latter? It's all nice talk but Mr. Johnny can't make us think we have not gained anything. O[h], poor Butler, how do they sell shoes if in Lowell?[3] At the present price I wonder how many pairs he would sell himself for. Guess he won't go <u>fishing</u> again until he's granted the privilege.

 I am enjoying good health, weight 155 pounds and growing.

        Good night,
        Your affectionate son and ____ brother
        T. J. Owen
        Acting Assistant Quartermaster
        Detachment
        50th New York Volunteer Engineers

The church that volunteer Engineers erected at Poplar Grove, near Petersburg, Virginia. *National Archives photograph 165-SB-74.*

46.   Detachment
        50th New York Volunteer Engineers
        near Poplar Grove Church, Virginia
        January 27th, 1865

Dear Father, Mother, and Sister,

    The last few days have been very busy times for us, and events have happened that we little dreamed of. On the 24th, we received a report that the enemy was making an attack on our lines in front and on the river. Many reports have been in circulation and as yet I am at a loss to know which is right. Without doubt, the enemy's gunboats tried to come down the river. Heavy firing has been heard in that direction and one thing is certain, they did not accomplish their object, which was undoubtedly to destroy our shipping at City Point and Bermuda Hundreds. (They say), that is, camp reports say, that five of the enemy's rams came down in the vicinity of Dutch Gap[1] where our heavy guns opened on them, that two of them ran aground, one exploded, and the other succeed[ed] in getting back up the stream.[2] This is good for what it's worth.

    Well, the same day, three of our companies were ordered to City Point to take charge of their pontons and be ready to move. About midnight, orders were received from headquarters, Army, that General Sheridan wanted a company of pontoniers, the same, if convenient, he had last summer (quite a compliment for Company I). Accordingly, the next morning, Brevet[3] Major Folwell, commanding Company I, made hasty preparations to go to the valley, and at noon, they left camp, bag and baggage, all feeling well pleased of again going with General P.H.S.[4] I was unable to go with them on account of the quartermaster business as all the train, animals, etc., were left with this Army. The anticipation is that they will take another train, and as soon as I can transfer my property and close the business, I am going to take charge of it. I hope to be able to get off the 30th as soon as I get through here. I shall go to Washington and there await orders.

    This may interfere with my calculations about coming home. Perhaps it will delay me some. At all events, I intend to come as soon as possible. Yesterday morning, I went to the [City] Point and saw the boys before they left. Major Folwell has received his full appointment and his brother, Brevet Captain Folwell, takes command of the company. He is a fine man and good officer, well liked by all. They left at 11 o'clock A.M. on the Steamer *Thomas Colyer*[5] for Annapolis, Maryland, where they will take the railroad to the Army of the Valley. Two of the companies that went to the [City] Point have come back. There is something in the wind though, yet.

Weather plenty cold.

> Very respectfully,
> Your obedient son and brother,
> Thomas J. Owen

47.

Detachment
50th New York Volunteer Engineers
near Poplar Grove Church, Virginia
February 7th, 1983 [1865]

Dear Friends at Home,

I am yet in my old quarters. Have been expecting to start for Washington for several days past, but since the late movement has taken place, there is no prospect of my getting away just now.

Sunday morning our troops began to move to the left and ere long the sound of battle told us they had met the enemy. The firing continued quite late in the evening. We were all packed up ready to move but none of the command was called for until nearly night. Then four companies (namely) C, D, H, and K were sent out with two days' rations under command of Brevet Major Van Brocklin, Company C.

I presume they have gone to fix roads or cut new ones as they took tools. Yesterday there was some firing in the afternoon. I went out to the tower which is now nearly done and took a good view of rebeldom from an elevation of 110 feet from the ground. I saw quite a number of ambulances going from the fight towards Petersburg. I presume they contained wounded. I also saw a train of cars on the Southside Railroad.[1]

Today there is some firing, though it is most to[o] stormy to do much at fighting. During the latter part of the night a nasty wet snow, about half rain, began to fall, but since morning it has turned altogether to rain an[d] still continues to descend.

Things have settled back as regards the move, and we now have no idea that we will break up winter quarters just now. What has been done, I am not able to say definitely. Therefore, will let you get the news from the papers and, by the [way], we have been very poorly supplied with that article lately, especially since the Potomac has been under ice. But, I have some idea that the late warm weather has thawed out the obstruction and that we will again be blessed with regular mails. That reminds me that I have not had a letter from you lately, but I presume I will find some in Washington as the company mail is now stopped there.

Talk about coming home well and that's about all, I guess you think by this time, but wait a little longer in hope.

With feelings of love and respect for you all.

I remain as ever,
Thomas

48.

Engineering Depot
Washington, D.C.
February 18th, 1865

My Dear Father, Mother, and Sister,

It is with feelings of the kindest regards that I sit down this pleasant evening to pen you a few lines in answer to your very kind letter of the 12th.

I am sorry to hear that mother is sick and sincerely hope she is better ere this. Indeed, I assure you nothing would give me more pleasure than to come home and spend a few days with you, but do not expect me just now. My business is so that I cannot possibly leave at present. After the train is all fitted out and we know what we are going to do and where we are going to do it, then I shall again think seriously about going north, that is if the compaign does not open earlier than usual. We are getting on nicely with the work. The weather is a little more mild just now and a few more such days as this will finish the snow. If one walks about, it's not

Engineer church and quarters, Fiftieth New York Volunteer Engineer Regiment, Poplar Grove, Virginia, March 1865. *Library of Congress photograph B817–7210.*

quite as pleasant under foot as might be, especially where there are no sidewalks. I was in the Capitol not long since and was much pleased with Powell's new picture, *Perry's Victory (on Lake Erie)*.[1] It is indeed a splendid painting. It hangs over the east door of the rotunda. Over the west door is a new and beautiful portrait of Major General <u>Grant</u>, life size.[2] The dome has been topped out since I saw it last winter[3] and now presents a very pleasing aspect.

    The city is as lively as usual and one would think from the number of officers and soldiers promenading Pennsylvania Avenue that the majority of the Army was on leave.

    O[h], I received a valentine the 14th and think I know the handwriting. I hope you received yours. The great peace question seems to have gradually died away and we all think more fighting must be done, ere the <u>little</u> gentlemen can see the folly of their ways. Well, if fight we must, let us do it with all our might, and those that survive this terrible struggle will never repent the time spent in so serious a cause. Would to God that every American citizen would look at this in its true light and realize the position we now hold. If there is a true born American that is willing to see this cruel war end here without the restoration of the <u>Union</u> and the <u>abolition</u> of <u>slavery</u> (the cursed cause of all this), I am ashamed of him. For my part, I feel the same warmth in the cause, and it seems to be just as much my duty to help what little I can as it did the day I first left home three years and a half ago. But this is enough now, you know my feelings as well as I can tell you. I have no doubt "if you did not," you do now.

                    Good night all,
                    I remain very respectfully your very obedient son,
                    Lieutenant Thomas J. Owen
                    Company I
                    50th New York Volunteer Engineers
                    Washington, D.C.

49.

White House, Virginia
March 19th, 1865

Dear Friends at Home,

In haste, I write a few lines to relieve the anxiety that you must have by this time. We arrived here yesterday, having been out 20 days without communication. In the meantime, we have traveled between 300 and 400 miles, near the latter. Left Winchester, 27th February. Moved down the Staunton Pike[1] to that place which we moved through on the morning of the 2d March. On the way, laid one bridge at Mount Jackson. Custer[2] had fight at Mount Crawford. Completely demolished Rosser's[3] command. From Staunton to Charlottesville rainy and muddy, very bad roads, mud [   ] deep. Had fight at Waynesborough. Swallowed Early's[4] whole command, he barely making his escape by rail from Charlottesville to the James River, which we struck at New Market. From New Market down the James by way of Scottsville to Columbia, we went most of the way on the towpath of the canal,[5] which we completely destroyed for nearly 100 miles from Columbia to Louisa Court House, where we again struck the Virginia Central Railroad[6] which we destroyed both here and at Charlottesville.

From Louisa Court House to this point by way of Chesterfield. March 20th morning, think of laying here a few days. All well.

Yours,
Thomas J. Owen

Ponton bridge over James River. *National Archives photograph 111-B-81.*

50.
                              Camp of Detachment
                              50th New York Volunteer Engineers
                              City Point, Virginia
                              March 30th, 1865

Dear Father, Mother, and Sister,

    As yet, I have no mail and I am living in great anxiety. I see by the papers that there has been very high water nearly all over the state. Therefore you must have had your share but I hope you are all safe.[1]
    We left White House on the 24th. Marched to the Chickahominy, which we bridged the same night. Next day, 25th, the corps crossed and we took up our bridges and marched to Harrison's Landing, where we stayed all night. 26th, marched up the river to Strawberry Plains. Crossed the James and camped for the night near Five Mile Creek[2] in the Army of the James.[3] 27th, marched to Hancock Station[4] on Grant's railroad and camped for the night. 28th, lay in camp. 29th, the Corps left at 3½ o'clock this morning with part of the train to join the cavalry expedition[5] on the left of the Army of the Potomac. About 7 o'clock, I received orders to send the remaining portion of the train to City Point. Marched to that place and went into park awaiting [orders] from Cavalry Corps headquarters. There is a big move going on. Last night we heard very heavy firing before Petersburg. Today has been rainy. Not much fighting within hearing.
    You may expect to hear great news. The rebellion is in its last reel and, within the next few months, will fall prostrate before the victorious armies of the U.S.[G].
    I am unable to say how long I will stay here. It may be a few day[s] and it may be months. I am very well indeed.

                              Yours truly,

                              Thomas J. Owen, 1st Lieutenant
                              50th New York Volunteer Engineers
                              and Acting Assistant Quartermaster

51.
                    Detachment
                    50th New York Volunteer Engineers
                    near City Point, Virginia
                    8 A.M., April 5th, 1865

Dear Friends at Home,

    In haste, I pen these few lines. Of late, there is so much news and so many victories that I hardly know what to say or where to begin, if I try.
    Yesterday, President "Lincoln" went up to Richmond, the steeples of which [I] plainly saw from the Howlett House Battery.[1] There is a report here that Lee has surrendered his whole army.
    Yesterday afternoon, I paid a visit to the Howlett House Battery up the James. This was the enemy's first work as you go up the river, and a good one it was. We found mounted one Brooke gun and the Columbiads, also one mortar.[2] They left things in great haste. The guns were spiked with nails[3] and can be extracted or drilled out whenever we wish to use them. This is a very sightly place. The crooked James is in view for several miles either way. Just below, lies [sic] the remains of the rebel ram,[4] near which and a little lower down were our obstructions which we have just blown out. Still farther down is Dutch Gap. Up the river, we trace the stream in its windings until it is lost among the trees and hills. While we were looking at this beautiful scenery, there appears in the distance two steamers winding their way down the James from Richmond, I presume, which shows that navigation is again open on the James.
    Just as we were about to leave, in came three Johnnys and gave themselves up, guns, accoutrements, and all. They were Virginians. Said they had been in the service since 1861. Had long wanted to get out but hated to desert, but now there was no hope. Respected General Lee but wanted to see Jeff Davis hung.[5] "That I find is the general sentiment." We brought them in and turned them over to the colonel of the 10th Artillery, New York.[6] I must now bid you good morning.
    No mail yet. I live in suspense. Have had none since the 25th February.

                    Yours truly,
                    Thomas J. Owen, 1st Lieutenant
                    50th New York Volunteer Engineers

52.

Camp of Detachment
50th New York Volunteer Engineers
City Point, Virginia
9:30 P.M., April 9th 1865

Dear Father, Mother, and Sister,

    We have just received the glorious news that General Lee has surrendered to our noble General Grant.

    A salute of heavy guns has just been fired. They sounded distant and were at Richmond, I think. The men all about here are cheering lustily and while I write, a salute is being fired here.

    11 o'clock P.M., I could not stand it any longer, I felt as though we ought to shout, so I turned out all hands, told them the news, and gave three cheers and such hearty ones. Oh, it did my very soul good. They then built a noble bonfire which is now blazing high and bright amid the shouts of the men, and well may they shout. Many of them have been with us through the trials and privations, exposed to the hardships of war ever since the summer of 1861, but thank God the day is nigh at hand when we can bid farewell to this <u>inhuman</u> life and return to our peaceful homes where anxious friends are waiting.

    We are all proud of this great and glorious event, proud that we are here and have participated in crushing out this wicked rebellion that came so near ruining our <u>glorious</u> and <u>noble government</u>. Thank god it is over now. We never shall see another such event for there will never be such an army to surrender again.

    It is a little less than a year since we left our winter quarters at Rappahannock. What has been achieved since, we all know. Many bloody battles have been fought and very many have fallen, but now those that survive reap the rewards, thanks to our noble leaders.

    I must now bid you good night. No mail yet.

                            Your very obedient and affectionate
                            son and brother,
                            Thomas J. Owen, 1st Lieutenant
                            50th New York Volunteer Engineers

53.	Camp of Detachment
50th New York Volunteer Engineers
City Point, Virginia
Easter Sunday, April 16th, 1865

Dear Father, Mother, and Sister,

Bad, o[h] very bad news today. I have just been to the [City] Point. A report is in circulation that President Lincoln was assassinated last Friday night, 14th, in Ford's Theatre by J[ohn] Wilkes Booth and died yesterday morning at 7 o'clock. Also, that Secretary Seward was assassinated in his own house.[1] This is all that is known but o[h], God, this is enough. A deep gloom rests upon us all. Flags are at half mast and everybody looks sad.

As I think of it, I can hardly believe it to be possible that the chief magistrate of the nation is dead. Still it must be so and I say to myself, what next? I almost tremble to think what may happen. Just at this present time, when the cloud of war seemed to be raising its dark mantle off us and we begin to see the sunshine of coming peace. Just while we are rejoicing over the late glorious victories that have been won under his most worthy administration. Just when he is wanted the most to finish up this terrible war not only for his good judgment but for his great experience in the affairs of the Government, he is "o[h]," I can hardly bear to mention it, "assassinated." Can it be possible? It almost makes my blood chill in my veins to think that there was such a fiend in human shape on the face of the earth, one that has derived benefit and protection from the Government. God forbid that he should ever be called an "American."

While I think of all this the great feelings of sorrow are almost overcome by a feeling of revenge, but that will not do. Now is the time we should control ourselves and look at things in their true light. This is the most critical time this Government ever saw and now is the time every American should rise up coolly and calmly, say in a determined manner the "law" must and shall be maintained, stand firm a little while and all will be well. Mr. Johnson[2] must be sustained by every true law abiding citizen (let us think what we will), but the public mind is laboring under such an excitement that we may expect almost anything. Let us be prepared for the worst and hope for the best. Take fate as it comes and be thankful it's no worse. Though it looks dark and gloomy now, the Nation will yet surmount the many obstacles that have beset it and come out brighter in the end.

Still no mail. The time seems long but there's no help for it so must endure it.

                      Your very obedient and affectionate son,
                      Thomas J. Owen, 1st Lieutenant
                      50th New York Volunteer Engineers

54.
                        Camp of Detachment
                        50th New York Volunteer Engineers
                        near City Point, Virginia
                        April 20th, 1865

Dear Father, Mother, and Sister,

    I still sing the same old song "no mail" yet but I am feeling well. The captain came back yesterday so that the whole of the company with this army is now here. We all feel well. The captain and his detachment have had pretty hard marching but met with very good luck. He says there was no train in the Army that moved as well as ours during the muddy time. On the left when everybody was sticking and floundering in the mire, he moved along without any trouble. This may not be of much interest to you folks at home but I merely mention it to let you know why I am feeling well. The detachment we left in Winchester were [sic] there when last heard from but we expect to get together again as soon as practicable. That is, we will either go to Washington where they will join us or have them come down here. There is a report in circulation that the regiment is going overland to Washington. Yesterday, they sent us an invitation to come out to (Burkeville) where they are and make the march with them. "Very fine thing." The men of the captain's detachment have only marched between 7 and 800 miles since 27th February and those of my detachment about 500 miles in the same time, and now spread eagles[1] at headquarters want us to come up and go with them on a pleasure excursion. I can call it nothing else because there is no enemy to chase or chase us and the idea of marching a couple of hundred miles just for the novelty of the thing is "played." However, I am going up to headquarters today and see what is going on. Think they are little hasty talking about going to Washington so soon. Don't see what is their great hurry unless it is to get there and have a "nigger show,"[2] which seems to be the zenith of their efforts just now, but this I guess is dead language for you. Never mind, I'll tell you all when the war is over.
    Lester Champlin arrived a day or two since from the "north." You would have laughed to see me question him and then wait in breathless anxiety for his answers but after all, didn't find out much. He said he had not been to our house since the "flood" but had heard that the house was partly turned round or tipped up on one side and here I am as anxious as ever. We have sent on to Washington to have the mail sent here at once, and I hope before I write again to know the full particulars of the inundation. It is "reported" here, by what authority I am unable to say, that Johnston[3] has followed the good example of General Lee. "Sound" if he has and "sound whipping" if he hasn't.

We have now and then a rainy day but the rest of the time is very pleasant. The "flies," those pretty little insects, have begun their hum in good earnest, and who would think it? They douse themselves into coffee, milk, ink, and everywhere you don't want them with the same impudence of their ancestors of last summer, but never mind, I guess there is room enough for us both, awhile, expecially as we talk strongly of evacuating and giving them full sway shortly.

As everybody says when they write letters, as for news, I have none. Perhaps you think I've told a story. I hope so.

I have not time to write anymore now. Neither do I wish to detain you longer with my nonsense, but I think the <u>best</u> way folks can wind up a letter is to tell the reader "as many do" that they can't think of "anything more," which I think is not much to "anyone's credit."

With my best wishes for all, I remain your very obedient son and brother,

      Thomas J. Owen, 1st Lieutenant
      50th New York Volunteer Engineers

P.S. Alice, please look and see (which I know you have ere this) whether in my last, I spelt the word assassin right.

      Tom

55.
                    Camp of Detachment
                    50th New York Volunteer Engineers
                    Middle Military Division[1]
                    Winchester, Virginia
                    May 2d, 1865

Dear Father, Mother, and Sister,

    Yours of the 9th April came to hand the 26th. I was then at City Point and until the present, have been so busy, that I have not had time to write. You remember that when we left there with General Sheridan, we left behind a detachment of the company and portion of the train under command of Lieutenant Bainbridge.[2]
    Well, after the marching was over, Richmond and Petersburg taken, and Lee surrendered, we settled down at City Point to await orders. In the meantime, we had heard nothing from those we left behind. Two months now elapsed, and we thought it best to try and get the company together. We applied to General Sheridan for an order to have the detachment at Winchester sent to City Point, but on account of Sherman's <u>blunder</u>,[3] he was sent immediately south with the companies before the order we requested had been issued. After talking the matter over with the captain, we came to the conclusion that I had better go to Winchester and see how matters stood. So on the morning of the 27th, I left City Point and arrived in Washington next day having had a fine trip. Stayed in Washington overnight. Did some business and telegraphed to Winchester to have my two months' back mail kept until I came. 29th, left Washington at 3 P.M. Arrived at Harpers Ferry about 9, same evening. Stayed there all night and took the 10 A.M. train for Stephenson,[4] where we arrived about noon. It was a lovely day (Sunday) and the scenery about, especially Harpers Ferry, was grand, but I have not time to tell you about mountains clothed in beautiful green as they were and rivers, waterfalls, rocks, etc. All these we must pass quickly by. At Stephenson, I got a horse and soon went the 4½ miles to Winchester, where I found the detachment in splendid condition. Corporal Jeff Ferguson, my forage master, had immediate charge of the animals and quartermaster property and has kept things in fine shape. M. Truman Smyth,[5] my clerk, has also done well. Everything is all right. The men are <u>all</u> well. Many of them were quite sick when we left and were left on that account, but the cool healthy climate and good water of this vicinity has been the making of them. It does me good to see how cheerful, healthy, and active they are. There is quite a difference between this climate and that of City Point. There, when I left it, was hot and dusty. The flies had began to be a nuisance, but here the air feels cool

and bracing. No flies. I am quite well pleased with the change. There is now only one thing that keeps me from being almost perfectly happy and that is my mail. (I know you will pity me.) My telegraph from Washington did not get here until after it had all been sent to City Point. You can imagine my disappointment.

How long we will remain here I am unable to say. General Hancock has sent another train here, which is under our charge. In all, we have a train of nearly 40 wagons beside that at City Point.

The captain telegraphed me this morning from City Point to return there immediately as he had orders to go to Washington, but we have orders here to bridge the Shenandoah tomorrow as some of the troops here are to be sent overland to Washington, so I think I had better stay and telegraphed the captain accordingly.

                Your obedient servant,
                Thomas J. Owen, 1st Lieutenant
                50th New York Volunteer Engineers

[Written on the margin] Enclosed please find ($50.00) Fifty Dollars.

NOTES TO LETTERS

Letter 1
1. "Friends at Home" refers to Owen's father, Thomas; mother, Almira; and younger sister, Alice. Numbers 27–31, page 402, Owego, Roll 867, Microcopy 653, *Eighth Census of the United States, 1860* (hereafter referred to as M653), Record Group 29, Records of the Bureau of the Census, National Archives Building (hereafter referred to as RG 29).
2. Camp Woodbury, named after the then commander of the Volunteer Engineer Brigade, Daniel P. Woodbury, was located in Alexandria, Virginia, near Fort Ward and the Fairfax Seminary. D.P. Woodbury to Captain Furgison, 9 April 1862, page 1, Volume 52/117 AP, Letters Sent, Volunteer Engineer Brigade, Army of the Potomac (hereafter referred to as LS, VEB, A of P), Record Group 393, Records of United States Army Continental Commands, 1821–1920, National Archives Building (hereafter referred to as RG 393) and Record of Events Cards (hereafter referred to as REC), Regimental Return, March 1862, Fiftieth New York Volunteer Engineer Regiment and Muster roll, March–April 1862, Company I, Fiftieth New York Volunteer Engineer Regiment, Roll 136, Microcopy 594, *Compiled Records Showing Service of Military Units in Volunteer Union Organizations* (hereafter referred to as M594), Record Group 94, Records of the Adjutant General's Office, National Archives Building (hereafter referred to as RG 94).
3. Apparently, Owen meant Manassas Junction on the Orange and Alexandria Railroad, which ran from Alexandria to Lynchburg, Virginia. Angus James Johnston III, *Virginia Railroads in the Civil War* (Chapel Hill, North Carolina: University of North Carolina Press, 1961), pp. 3–4 and 257, fn. 4.
4. Fortress, actually Fort, Monroe, first garrisoned in 1823, is located at Point Comfort, Virginia, between the York and James rivers. Francis Paul Prucha, *A Guide to the Military Posts of the United States 1789–1895* (Madison, Wisconsin: The State Historical Society of Wisconsin, 1964), p. 92.
5. Colonel J. McLeod Murphy commanded the Fiftieth New York Volunteer Engineer Regiment. War Department, *The War of the Rebellion: A Compilation of the Official Records of the Union and Confederate Armies* (Washington, DC: Government Printing Office, 1880–1901) (hereafter referred to as *Official Records, Army*), Series I, Volume II, Part I, p. 134.
6. The steamer *Louisiana* transported the Fiftieth New York Volunteer Engineer Regiment from Alexandria to Ship Point, Virginia, 9–11 April 1862. Congress, *House Executive Document No. 337, Vessels Bought, Sold, and Chartered by the United States, 1861–68* (40th Cong., 2d sess.) (hereafter referred to as *Vessels Bought*), pp. 58–59, and REC, Regimental Return, April 1862, Fiftieth New York Volunteer Engineer Regiment and Morning Report, April 1862, Fiftieth New York Volunteer Engineer Regiment, Roll 136, M594, RG 94.
7. No information pertaining to "Putt," probably a nickname, could be found.

Letter 2
1. Harrison's Landing, on the James River, was the headquarters and supply base for McClellan's army from 3 July–16 August 1862. Mark M. Boatner, *The Civil War Dictionary* (New York: David McKay Company, Inc., 1959), p. 379. For the location of Harrison's Landing, *see* War Department, *Atlas to Accompany the Official Records of the Union and Confederate Armies*

(Washington, DC: Government Printing Office, 1891-1895) (hereafter referred to as *Official Atlas*).
2. "Cesesh" was slang for Confederates.
3. The "big battle" took place at Cedar Mountain, Virginia, on 9 August 1862, where Thomas "Stonewall" Jackson's Confederate forces defeated some of John Pope's Union troops under the command of Nathaniel Banks. Pope, formerly a Topographical Engineer officer, became commander of the Army of Virginia on 26 June 1862 and suffered a severe defeat at Second Manassas, 29-30 August 1862. Boatner, *Civil War Dictionary*, pp. 101-105 and 653-659.
4. *Frank Leslie's Illustrated* was a popular newspaper/magazine during the Civil War with a format similar to *Harper's Weekly*.

Letter 4
1. Stoneman's Station was a stop on the Aquia and Fredericksburg Railroad, which carried supplies and men from Aquia Creek on the Potomac to Falmouth on the Rappahannock River. James A. Huston, *The Sinews of War: Army Logistics 1775-1923* (Washington, DC: Government Printing Office, 1966), pp. 223-224.
2. Philip R. Goodrich mustered in as a first sergeant in Company I, Fiftieth New York Engineers, on 26 August 1861, received a promotion to second lieutenant on 11 December 1862, and resigned from the service on 4 May 1863. Company I, Fiftieth New York Volunteer Engineer Regiment, Descriptive Books of Volunteer Organizations: Civil War, 1861-65 (hereafter referred to as Co. I, 50th, DB), RG 94, and Frederick Phisterer, Compiler, *New York in the War of the Rebellion 1861 to 1865* (Albany: J.B. Lyon Company, 1912), p. 1679.
3. Before promotion to second lieutenant on 11 December 1862, Philip R. Goodrich was orderly sergeant of Company I. Owen filled the vacancy when promoted to first sergeant on 2 February 1863. Thomas J. Owen, Compiled Military Service Record, Fiftieth New York Volunteer Engineer Regiment, Carded Records, Volunteer Organizations: Civil War (hereafter referred to as CMSR), RG 94.
4. Major General Joseph Hooker was commander of the Army of the Potomac, 26 January-28 June 1863. Boatner, *Civil War Dictionary*, pp. 409-410.
5. Major General Ambrose Burnside, who directed the disastrous assault on Fredericksburg, 13 December 1862, commanded the Army of the Potomac, 10 November 1862-26 January 1863. George W. Cullum, *Biographical Register of the Officers and Graduates of the U.S. Military Academy*. . . (Boston: Houghton Mifflin and Company, 1891), Volume 2, p. 317.
6. "Little Mac" was George B. McClellan, an Engineer officer in the Army before the Civil War, who commanded the Army of the Potomac in the Peninsula and Antietam campaigns and was generally admired by the average soldier. Boatner, *Civil War Dictionary*, p. 524.

Letter 5
1. Augustus S. Perkins mustered into the service on 18 December 1861 as a first lieutenant in Company I and received a promotion to captain on 18 July 1862. He was killed on 11 December 1862 at Fredericksburg, Virginia, by Confederate rifle fire while attempting to erect a ponton bridge over the Rappahannock River. Co. I, 50th, DB, RG 94; and Phisterer, *New York*, pp. 1684-85.
2. Mustered into the service as a private in Company I on 26 August 1861, Hanson G. Champlin died on 11 December 1862 at Fredericksburg, Virginia,

from enemy rifle fire while laying a ponton bridge across the Rappahannock River. Co. I, 50th, DB; and Hanson G. Champlin, CMSR, RG 94.
3. Fredericksburg, Virginia.
4. Joseph Hooker appointed Brigadier General Henry W. Benham commander of the Volunteer Engineer Brigade on 20 March 1863. *Official Records, Army*, Series I, Volume 25, Part II, p. 150 (Special Order No. 78, Army of the Potomac, 20 March 1863).

Letter 6
1. For other accounts and information relating to these Engineer operations at Franklin's Crossing on 5 June 1863, see Gilbert Thompson, *The Engineer Battalion in the Civil War*, Occasional Papers No. 44 (Washington, DC: Press of the Engineer School, 1910), pp. 34-35, and *Official Records, Army*, Series I, Volume 27, Part I, pp. 32-33 and 676-677, and Part III, p 63.
2. Civil War historian Bell I. Wiley theorized that the sobriquet "Johnny Reb" or "Johnny" resulted from Union soldiers yelling out "Hello Johnny" to Confederate combatants opposing them. Bell I. Wiley, *The Life of Johnny Reb* (Indianapolis, Indiana: Bobbs-Merrill Company, Inc., 1943), p. 13.
3. A ponton, or pontoon, as it was spelled during the Civil War, was a flat-bottomed vessel or similar object, constructed of wood or canvas, used to support a temporary or ponton bridge on which men and supplies could cross a body of water. For drawings of canvas ponton boats and bridges, see Number 1, Plat 106, in *Official Atlas*. Boatner, *Civil War Dictionary*, p. 658, and John S. Scott, *A Dictionary of Civil Engineering* (Hammondsworth, England: Penquin Books, Ltd., 1958), p. 268.
4. William Watts Folwell received a commission as first lieutenant in Company G on 13 February 1862. Promoted to captain in Company I on 12 December 1862, he became a major on 1 February 1865. Breveted a lieutenant colonel in the U.S. Volunteers on 9 April 1865, Folwell mustered out of the service on 13 June 1865. Co. I, 50th DB, RG 94; Phisterer, *New York*, p. 1679; and Allen Johnson and Dumas Malone, *Dictionary of American Biography* (New York: Charles Scribner's Sons, 1927-1973) (hereafter referred to as *DAB*), Volume 3, pp. 495-496.
5. The "Minie ball," a cylindroconical rifle bullet with an expanding base, was used in Civil War shoulder arms and handguns. Captain Claude E. Minie of the French Army, who improved upon the original "Minie ball," lent his name to this invention of Captain John Norton of the British Army. John Quick, *Dictionary of Weapons and Military Terms* (New York: McGraw-Hill Book Company, 1973), p. 307; and Bernard and Fawn Brodie, *From Crossbow to H-Bomb* (Revised and Enlarged Edition, Bloomington, Indiana: Indiana University Press, 1973), p. 132.
6. Major General John Sedgwick commanded the Sixth Army Corps of the Army of the Potomac on 5 June 1863. A graduate of the U.S. Military Academy in 1837, Sedgwick remained in the Army until his death on 9 May 1864, mortally wounded by a Confederate sharpshooter at Spotsylvania Court House. Boatner, *Civil War Dictionary*, pp. 730-731.
7. Mustered in as a captain of Company E on 29 August 1861, Ira Spaulding received a commission as major on 14 October 1862 and as lieutenant colonel on 1 January 1864. Before mustering out of the service on 13 June 1865, he received brevet commissions as colonel on 1 April 1864 and as brigadier general on 9 April 1865. Ira Spaulding, CMSR, RG 94; and Phisterer, *New York*,

p. 1687.
8. John E. Armstrong mustered into service on 6 September 1861 and reported to Company F. He transferred to Company I on 1 November 1861. Armstrong received a promotion to corporal on 2 February 1863. At the expiration of his service, he mustered out on 20 September 1864. John E. Armstrong, CMSR, and Co. I, 50th, DB, RG 94.
9. Calvin Q. Newcome mustered in as a private in Company F on 27 August 1862. He received a promotion to sergeant on 8 October 1862 and a commission as first lieutenant in Company C on 28 February 1863. Newcome resigned his commission on 30 July 1864. Phisterer, *New York*, p. 1684.

Letter 7
1. "Old Ground" refers to the former Camp Lesley, which by the date of this letter had become the Washington Engineer Depot.
2. Information pertaining to these operations can be found in *Official Records, Army*, Series I, Volume 27, Part III, p. 527.
3. The identity of "Ely" is unknown.
4. The identity of "Longstreet" is unknown. William Lay, Jr., of the Tioga (New York) County Historical Society wrote that such a street did not exist in Owego during the Civil War. Apparently, Owen was not referring to James Longstreet, a Confederate general in the Army of Northern Virginia, either. In September 1863, Longstreet and his command left the East for Tennessee, but that was long after Owen wrote his letter.

Letter 8
1. For more information pertaining to the operations of the Fiftieth New York Volunteer Engineer Regiment following the Battle of Gettysburg, see Paul H. Thienel, "Engineers in the Union Army 1861–1865," *The Military Engineer* 47 (January–February 1955), p. 40.
2. Owen is referring to the Chesapeake and Ohio Canal, which ran from Cumberland, Maryland, to the District of Columbia. *Dictionary of American History* (Revised Edition, New York: Charles Scribner's Sons, 1976), Volume 2, p. 15. *See also* Walter L. Sanderlin, *The Great National Project: A History of the Chesapeake and Ohio Canal* (Baltimore: The Johns Hopkins Press, 1946); and National Park Service, *Chesapeake and Ohio Canal, Maryland* (Washington, DC: Government Printing Office, 1942).
3. Henry LaGrange mustered into Company I as a corporal on 26 August 1861. Promoted to sergeant on 21 January 1862, he received commissions as second lieutenant in Company I on 20 June 1864 and first lieutenant on 22 September 1864. LaGrange mustered out of the service on 13 June 1865. Co. I, 50th, DB, and Henry LaGrange, CMSR, RG 94; and Phisterer, *New York*, p. 1681.
4. On 3 March 1863, Congress passed "an Act for Enrolling and Calling Out the National Forces, and for other purposes," which was, in effect, the first national draft in the United States. The first enrollment occurred in May 1863 and the first draft in early July. Many individuals opposed the draft because they were sure it was unfair, and some rioting resulted, especially in New York City. Owen was concerned that riots might occur in Washington, D.C., and his unit would then respond to the emergency. Marvin A. Kreidberg and Merton G. Henry, *History of Military Mobilization in the United States Army 1775–1945* (Washington, DC: Government Printing Office, 1955), pp. 104–109.

Letter 9
1. In the provisions of the 3 March 1863 Enrollment Act, a drafted man could pay the War Department up to $300.00 to procure a substitute for him. Kreidberg and Henry, *Military Mobilizations*, pp. 111-113.

Letter 10
1. No information pertaining to Cousin Lucretia could be found.
2. Enrolled at Owego on 14 August 1861, George Forsyth became a musician in Company I, Fiftieth New York Volunteer Engineer Regiment. Promoted to drum major as of 1 November 1861, he transferred to the noncommissioned officer staff. Reduced to musician on 18 September 1862, he received a medical discharge from the Army on 3 April 1863 following a lengthy illness. George Forsyth, CMSR, RG 94.
3. Starting on 10 July 1863, Quincy A. Gillmore, commander of the Department of the South, commenced an artillery bombardment of the Confederate-occupied fortifications in Charleston Harbor. At 1:30 on the morning of 22 August, Union troops started firing on the city of Charleston itself. Gillmore hoped to force the city and its defenses to surrender quickly but the U.S. forces did not occupy Charleston until 18 February 1865. *Official Records, Army*, Series I, Volume 28, Part I, pp. 3-39, 201-202, 225-239, 597-679, and 682-684, and Part II, pp. 51-52 and 58-59; and Volume 47, Part I, pp. 1019-20. E. Milby Burton, *The Siege of Charleston, 1861-1865* (Columbia, South Carolina: University of South Carolina Press, 1970), pp. 251-254; and Frank Barnes, *Fort Sumter* (Washington, DC: Government Printing Office, 1962), pp. 26-28.
4. South Carolina, in which Charleston is located, was the first state to secede from the Union. Also, most authorities contend that the Civil War began when secessionists in Charleston commenced firing on Fort Sumter in the harbor on 12 April 1861. Thus, Owen, like many others, blamed the citizens of Charleston for causing the Civil War. Boatner, *Civil War Dictionary*, pp. 299-300.
5. Apparently, Owen is referring to the New York City draft riots that occurred in July 1963. Protests against the draft ensued elsewhere in the state.

Letter 11
1. The Eleventh Corps of the Army of the Potomac, constituted on 12 September 1862, included a large number of German-speaking soldiers. Routed by Stonewall Jackson's men at Chancellorsville and again by other Confederate troops at Gettysburg, the corps transferred to the Army of the Cumberland on 25 September 1863, the day that Owen saw it at Fairfax Station. Boatner, *Civil War Dictionary*, p. 193.
2. The 137th New York Volunteer Infantry Regiment, organized at Binghamton, New York, mustered into federal service on 25 September 1862. Serving with the Army of the Cumberland until the fall of 1863, the regiment then transferred to the Army of the Cumberland and remained with it until the end of the war. Fredrick B. Dyer, *A Compendium of the Rebellion* (Reprint, New York: Thomas Yoseloff, Publisher, 1959), Volume 3, p. 1457.
3. Constituted in September of 1862 in the Army of the Potomac, the Twelfth Army Corps transferred to the Army of the Cumberland in September of 1863. In April of 1864, the corps, along with the Eleventh, became part of the Twentieth. Boatner, *Civil War Dictionary*, p. 194.

Letter 12
1. John Frear mustered into Company H, Third New York Volunteer Infantry Regiment, on 14 May 1861 and left the service on 21 May 1863. John Frear, CMSR, RG 94.

Letter 13
1. A corduroy bridge included a roadbed constructed of wooden logs laid crosswise.
2. Major General George Gordon Meade, a former Engineer officer, was commander of the Army of the Potomac from 28 June 1863 to the end of the war. Johnson and Malone, *DAB*, Volume 6, pp. 474–476.
3. Following the initial draft in July 1863, President Lincoln called for 300,000 three-year volunteers on 17 October and warned that if he did not get them, he would conduct a new draft on 5 January 1864. Later, the President postponed the draft until 15 April 1864. Kreidberg and Henry, *Military Mobilization*, pp. 106–108.

Letter 14
1. Discharged from the service on 26 December 1863 to reenlist as a veteran volunteer, Owen received a new bounty and 35 days' furlough. His furlough lasted from 29 December 1863 to 1 February 1864. Thomas J. Owen, CMSR, RG 94.
2. Ira Spaulding enrolled on 5 August 1861 at Niagara, New York, and mustered into federal service as a captain, commanding Company E, on 29 August 1861. On 8 August 1862, he transferred to Company F, became a major on 14 October 1862, and received a promotion to lieutenant colonel on 1 January 1864. Breveted a brigadier general of U.S. Volunteers to date from 9 April 1865, he mustered out of the service on 14 June 1865. Phisterer, *New York*, p. 1687, and Boatner, *Civil War Dictionary*, p. 781.
3. Major General John Newton, a Corps of Engineers officer in peacetime and Chief of Engineers from 6 March 1884 to 27 August 1886, commanded the First Corps, Army of the Potomac, from 2 July 1863 to 24 March 1864. Boatner, *Civil War Dictionary*, p. 593.
4. The First Corps, constituted in the Army of the Potomac on 13 September 1862, existed until March of 1864, when its strength was so small because of casualties that the remaining men were transferred to the Second, Fifth, and Sixth corps. Boatner, *Civil War Dictionary*, pp. 187–188.

Letter 15
1. "Lords of Creation" apparently refers to the rich plantation owners.
2. Edmund C. Pritchett, the chaplain of the regiment, was in Washington, D.C., in February of 1864. Phisterer, *New York*, p. 1685; and Regimental Returns, January and February 1864, Fiftieth New York Volunteer Engineer Regiment; and Muster Rolls, 31 December 1863–9 February 1864, Field and Staff, Fiftieth New York Volunteer Engineer Regiment, from Muster Rolls of Volunteer Organizations: Civil War, Mexican War, Creek War, Cherokee Removal, and Other Wars, 1863–1865 (hereafter referred to as MRs), RG 94.
3. Apparently, "beautiful emblem of the Union" refers to the United States flag flying above the various camps of the many Army units in the area.
4. Mustered in as a private in Company I on 6 September 1861, John W. Bunzey became an artificer in 1863 and received a promotion to corporal on 23 March

1864. Bunzey mustered out of the service on 13 June 1865. Co. I, 50th, DB, and John W. Bunzey, CMSR, RG 94.

Letter 16
1. The cause of George Forsyth's death could not be found.

Letter 17
1. Almost three-fourths of the men in the Fiftieth New York Volunteer Engineer Regiment reenlisted for the remainder of the war during the winter of 1863–1864. However, under new legislation, the regiment was authorized 12 companies of 150 men each, and needed many recruits and additional officers. Owen hoped to receive a commission as an officer but he was afraid that not enough men would enlist to justify his promotion. Actually, the regiment received more than enough recruits. New York State Monuments Commission for the Battlefields of Gettysburg and Chattanooga, *Final Report on the Battlefield of Gettysburg* (Albany: J.B. Lyon Company, 1902) (hereafter referred to as NYSMC, *Final Report*), Volume 3, pp. 1093–94.

Letter 18
1. Lester Champlin enlisted as a private on 2 January 1864 and joined Company I in Virginia on 25 February. He mustered out of the service on 13 June 1865. Lester Champlin, CMSR, RG 94.
2. After enlisting in the service on 4 January 1864, Frederick Hunt joined Company I in Virginia on 25 February. On 13 June 1865, he mustered out of the service. Frederick Hunt, CMSR, RG 94.
3. More than enough men enlisted in the Fiftieth New York Volunteer Engineer Regiment, and the Fifteenth New York Volunteer Engineer Regiment organized four full companies from the surplus recruits. NYSMC, *Final Report*, Volume 3, p. 1094.
4. On the back of the photograph (carte de visite) of Owen that appears in this publication is the inscription "J. Berry, Photographer, Owego, N.Y." Most likely, the photograph mentioned by Owen is the same as the one reproduced here.
5. Jefferson Ferguson mustered into Company I as a private on 26 August 1861. Later an artificer, he then received a promotion to corporal on 5 May 1864 and mustered out of the service on 13 June 1865. Co. I, 50th, DB, and Jefferson Ferguson, CMSR, RG 94.
6. Mustered into the service as a sergeant in Company I on 26 August 1861, Albert B. Beers was reduced to a private on 1 December 1863 for gambling. Promoted to artificer on 1 April 1864, he mustered out of the service on 26 August 1865. Co. I, 50th, DB, and Albert B. Beers, CMSR, RG 94.

Letter 19
1. Among the Owen Papers in the custody of the Historical Division, Office, Chief of Engineers, is a letter, dated 18 April 1864, in which Milicent refers to Thomas J. Owen as "my younger brother." In both the 1850 and 1860 National Censuses, the Owens listed three children—Mary, the oldest; Thomas; and Alice, the youngest. The 1840 National Census and the ones preceding it did not list children. Thus, Milicent could be a much older sister, possibly 20 or more years older than Thomas, or Mary may have adopted the name Milicent. Thomas J. Owen Papers, Historical Division, Office, Chief of Engineers,

Washington, D.C., and Numbers 5-8, p. 257, Owego, Roll 604, Microcopy 432, *Seventh Census of the United States, 1850* (hereafter referred to as M432), and Numbers 27-31, p. 402, Owego Roll 867, M653, RG 29.

2. For a map showing the location of Yorktown batteries 1 and 4, see *Official Atlas*, Plate 14, Map 1. Battery No. 1, at Farinholt's (Farenholdt) House on the right bank of Wormley's Creek at its junction with the York River, eventually mounted two 200-pound and five 100-pound Parrott guns. Battery No. 4, at Moore's House in a ravine under the plateau, mounted ten 12-inch seacoast mortars. *Official Records, Army*, Series I, Volume II, Part I, pp. 272, 318-319, 324, 331, 334, and 339-340; and Thienel, "Engineers in the Union Army," p. 38.

3. As he often did, Owen left out a world between "large" and "in." Perhaps Owen meant to include the word "gun."

Letter 20

1. The Army of the Potomac received many reports of enemy movements on 17 and 18 March 1864. See *Official Records, Army*, Series I, Volume 33, pp. 687-696.

2. Lieutenant General Ulysses Simpson Grant became the commander of the Armies of the United States on 12 March 1864, a position he held until after the Civil War was over. Instead of staying in Washington, D.C., to direct the various Union military operations, Grant made his headquarters in the field with the Army of the Potomac. Boatner, *Civil War Dictionary*, pp. 352-353.

3. "U.S.," an abbreviation for Ulysses Simpson, refers to Grant, Commanding General of the Armies of the United States.

Letter 22

1. Most officers in volunteer organizations received commissions from the governors of their states. The method of selecting officers in volunteer organizations varied from unit to unit and with the dates of appointment. Early in the war, the rank and file often elected their officers, but later on, examining boards or other officers recommended them. On 17 March 1864, Company I finally had its full complement of 150 men, which created additional new vacancies for officers. Owen received his 30 March 1864 commission, signed by the Democratic Governor Horatio Seymour, as second lieutenant on 16 April, assumed duties in the company on 18 April, mustered for promotion on 27 April, and mustered in as a commissioned officer to date from 28 April. On 1 October 1888, Owen applied for his date of rank as second lieutenant to be redesignated as 17 March 1864 because an original vacancy occurred on that date. The company reached its full complement on 17 March and another officer, technically promoted to first lieutenant on that day, left an additional vacancy. The Adjutant General of the United States Army approved Owen's request, and officially the date of rank became 17 March 1864. William H. Pettes to C. Clapp, 19 April 1864, Regimental Papers, Fiftieth New York Volunteer Engineer Regiment, MRs, 1836-1865; Thomas J. Owen, CMSR; and 13015 VS 1865, Letters Received, Volunteer Service Division (hereafter referred to as LS, VSD), RG 94; Boatner, *Civil War Dictionary*, p. 733; Kreidberg and Henry, *Military Mobilization*, pp. 115-119; Fred Albert Shannon, *The Organization and Administration of the Union Army 1861-1865* (Cleveland, Ohio: The Arthur H. Clarke Company, 1928), Volume I, pp. 157-160; and Leonard L. Lerwill, *The Personnel Replacement System in the United States Army* (Washington, DC:

Government Printing Office, 1954), pp. 121-123.
2. Private William H. Kipp of Company I died on 10 April 1864 at Rappahannock Station, Virginia, of remittent fever. Co. I, 50th, DB, RG 94.
3. Artificer Aaron Fridley of Company I died on 13 April 1864 at Rappahannock Station, Virginia, from debility following measles. Co. I, 50th, DB, RG 94.

Letter 23
1. Mahlon Bainbridge Folwell, brother of William Watts Folwell, mustered into the Fiftieth New York Volunteer Engineer Regiment as a hospital steward on 10 April 1862. Promoted to first lieutenant in Company I on 19 May 1863, he succeeded his brother as captain and commanding officer on 1 February 1865 and mustered out of the service on 13 June 1865. Co. I, 50th, DB, and Mahlon Bainbridge Folwell, CMSR, RG 94; and Phisterer, *New York*, p. 1679.
2. William H. Pettes, a graduate of the U.S. Military Academy at West Point, served in the Regular Army from 1832 to 1836 before resigning his commission. Mustered into the Fiftieth New York Volunteer Engineer Regiment as a lieutenant colonel on September 1861, Pettes became a colonel commanding the regiment on 3 June 1863. He mustered out of the service on 5 July 1865. Phisterer, *New York*, p. 1685; and Francis B. Heitman, *Historical Register and Dictionary of the United States Army*. . .(Reprint, Urbana, Illinois: University of Illinois Press, 1965), Volume 1, p. 786.

Letter 24
1. Francis Bacon mustered in as a private in Company I on 28 August 1862 and received a promotion to sergeant on 1 November 1862. Transferring to Company D, Bacon received commissions as second lieutenant on 13 March 1864 and first lieutenant on 21 September 1864. He mustered out of the service on 13 June 1865. Special Order No. 10, Headquarters, Detachment, Engineer Brigade, Rappahannock Station, Virginia, 22 March 1864, directed Captain W.W. Folwell and Sergeants Thomas J. Owen and Francis Bacon to proceed to Washington, D.C., on 24 March as witnesses in a general court martial convened at the headquarters of the Engineer Brigade. Regimental Papers, Fiftieth New York Volunteer Engineer Regiment, MRs, 1836-1865, and Co. I, 50th, DB, RG 94; and Phisterer, *New York*, p. 1675.
2. George W. Marshall, mustered into Company I as a private on 28 August 1862, deserted from camp near Falmouth, Virginia, on 18 January 1863. After apprehension, he was court martialed, found guilty, and sentenced to be shot to death, but the court unanimously recommended mercy. Generals Benham and Meade also recommended mercy, which President Lincoln approved. Marshall was imprisoned on Dry Tortugas at hard labor to work on fortifications and other tasks. In June 1865, he received a dishonorable discharge from the Army and was released from custody. Co. I, 50th, DB, and George W. Marshall, CMSR, RG 94, and M1394, Proceedings of General Court Martials, Record Group 153, Records of the Office of the Judge Advocate General (Army), National Archives Building.
3. Located at 11 South A Street, across from the Capitol grounds between 1st Street East and New Jersey Avenue, the Casparis Hotel functioned as a hostelry and a hospital during the Civil War. District of Columbia, Part II, Indexes to Field Records of Hospitals, 1821-1912, RG 94, p. 8, and Map 1, Sequence A, Sheet 44, Post and Reservation File, Record Group 92, Records of the Office of the Quartermaster General, National Archives Building (hereafter re-

ferred to as RG 92).
4. Originally installed in the Capitol in November 1863, the bronze door, modeled by Randolph Rogers in Rome, Italy, in 1858, was cast in Munich, Germany, by Ferdinand von Miller at the Royal Bavaria Foundry in 1861. Presently located at the eastern entrance to the rotunda in the Capitol, this two-valve door includes eight panels depicting various events in the life of Christopher Columbus. Architect of the Capitol, *Compilation of Works of Art and Other Objects in the United States Capitol* (Washington, DC: Government Printing Office, 1965), pp. 368–369.
5. Apparently, Owen attended the Trinity Episcopal Church, located at the corner of 3rd Street West and C Street North. *Washington: What to See and How to See It* (Washington, DC: Philip and Solomons, 1860), p. 11; and William F. Richstein, *The Stranger's Guide-book to Washington City and Everybody's Pocket Handy-book* (Washington, DC: William F. Richstein, 1864), p. 83.
6. Cornelius M. Pierce mustered into Company I as a corporal, was promoted to sergeant on 23 March 1864, and mustered out on 13 June 1865. Cornelius M. Pierce, CMSR, RG 94.
7. Following his muster-in on 26 August 1861, Orvin L. Newell was promoted to corporal in January 1862 and sergeant on 23 March 1864, and mustered out of the service on 13 June 1865 after spending his entire career in Company I. Orvin L. Newell, CMSR, RG 94.
8. Originally mustered into Company K as a private on 18 September 1861, Charles R. Bodle transferred to Company I on 1 November 1861, received promotions to corporal on 1 September 1862 and sergeant on 23 March 1864, and mustered out of the service on 13 June 1865. Charles R. Bodle, CMSR, RG 94.
9. Smith Surdam, originally mustered in as a private in Company D, transferred to Company I on 1 November 1861, became a corporal on 22 June 1862 and sergeant on 23 March 1864, and mustered out on 13 June 1865. Smith Surdam, CMSR, RG 94.
10. James H. Perkins mustered into Company I on 7 September 1861 as a private, became an artificer in the spring of 1863 and corporal on 23 March 1863, and died of illness on 6 October 1864. James H. Perkins, CMSR, RG 94.
11. Mustered into Company I as a private on 26 August 1861, Theodore F. Probasco received a promotion to corporal on 26 October 1862 but reverted back to his original rank on 24 December 1862 for absence without leave. Again promoted to corporal on 23 March 1864, Probasco became a sergeant on 8 October 1864 and mustered out of the service on 13 June 1865. Theodore F. Probasco, CMSR, RG 94.
12. Caleb LaGrange mustered into Company I on 6 September 1862 as a private, became an artificer in the spring of 1863 and corporal on 23 March 1864, and mustered out on 13 June 1865. Caleb LaGrange, CMSR, RG 94.
13. For the location of Hazel Run, see *Official Atlas*, Plate 32, Map 2.

Letter 25
1. Zoan Church was sometimes referred to as Zion or Zoar Church. See *Official Atlas*, Plate 39, Maps 2 and 3; Plate 41, Map 1; Plate 45, Map 1; Plate 47, Map 6; and Plate 93, Map 2.
2. Brigadier General David McMurtie Gregg, a graduate of the U.S. Military Academy at West Point in 1855, commanded the Second Division, Cavalry Corps, Army of the Potomac, when Owen saw him at Kelly's Ford on 29 March 1864. Boatner, *Civil War Dictionary*, p. 357.

3. Organized in March 1862, the Second Corps served continuously with the Army of the Potomac from 12 September 1862 until June 1865. Boatner, *Civil War Dictionary*, pp. 188-189.

4. Major General Gouverneur Kemble Warren, an Engineer officer for almost all of his Army career, commanded the Second Corps during 2 September-16 December 1863, 29 December 1863-9 January 1864, and 15 January-24 March 1864. However, on 5 May 1864, Warren commanded the Fifth Corps. Boatner, *Civil War Dictionary*, p. 891.

5. Located just east of the junction of the Orange Turnpike and the Germana Road on the Wilderness Battlefield, the Old Wilderness Tavern was a deserted building partially obstructed from view by weeds and trees when Owen saw it. Horace Porter, *Campaigning With Grant* (Bloomington, Indiana: Indiana University Press, 1961), p. 49.

6. Artificer Beldon Allen of Company E was wounded in the head by a shell while in the rifle pits on 6 May 1864. Not seriously injured, Allen continued to serve with his company throughout the war. Beldon Allen, CMSR, and Muster Roll, 30 April-30 June 1864, Company E, Fiftieth New York Volunteer Engineer Regiment, MRs, 1836-1865, RG 94.

7. The exact identification of Bensen's Farm is unknown but it may be the property down the Rapidan River from Ely's Ford shown on Maps 2 and 3, Plate 39, in the *Official Atlas*.

8. Second lieutenants in the Corps of Engineers, cavalry, light artillery, and ordance received $53.33 per month. Infantry and artillery second lieutenants earned $45.00 each month. Examination of numerous regulations and orders failed to disclose any stipulation that Engineer officers had to have horses but they were paid the same as mounted officers. Pay Department (War Department), *A Compendium of the Pay of the Army from 1785 to 1888* (Washington, DC: Government Printing Office, 1888), pp. 42, 44-45, and 48-49, and Adjutant General's Office, *Official Army Register* (Washington, DC: Government Printing Office, 1864), pp. 112-115.

Letter 26

1. Impressed by the work of the British Sanitary Commission in the Crimean War, individuals interested in the health of the Civil War soldiers influenced the Secretary of War, Simon Cameron, to issue an order on 9 June 1861 which established the United States Sanitary Commission. Through its various branches, the United States Sanitary Commission supplemented diets, cared for the wounded, established lodges for transient soldiers at railroad depots and a home for discharged soldiers in Washington, D.C., and compiled a list of hospitals. Kenneth W. Munden and Henry Putney Beers, *Guide to Federal Archives Relating to the Civil War* (Washington, DC: Government Printing Office, 1962), pp. 587-588; and Boatner, *Civil War Dictionary*, p. 720.

2. Most likely, Owen is referring to the Richmond, Fredericksburg, and Potomac Railroad. This railroad ran 75 miles from Aquia Creek on the Potomac River to Richmond, Virginia. Johnston, *Virginia Railroads,* p. 4.

3. Major General Winfield Scott Hancock, a graduate of the U.S. Military Academy at West Point in 1840, commanded the Second Corps of the Army of the Potomac on 21 May 1864. Boatner, *Civil War Dictionary*, p. 372.

4. Originally mustered in as the Ira Harris Cavalry between August and October 1861, the Fifth New York Volunteer Cavalry Regiment, designated as such on 14 November 1861, recruited in the New York City area. Assigned

at first to the Washington, D.C., area, the regiment later served with the Army of the Potomac and the Army of the Shenandoah. Dyer, *A Compendium*, Volume 3, pp. 1373-74.
5. A graduate of the U.S. Military Academy at West Point in 1853, Major General Philip Henry Sheridan commanded the Cavalry Corps of the Army of the Potomac in June of 1864. Boatner, *Civil War Dictionary*, pp. 747-748.
6. Huntley's Crossing was on the Pamunkey River about four miles northwest of Hanover Town, Virginia. The crossing is marked as Hundley's in *Official Atlas*, Plate 92, Map 1, Section 2. *See also* Thienel, "Engineers in the Union Army," p. 41; and Thompson, *Engineer Battalion*, p. 63.
7. The land in Virginia between the York River and James River at the mouth of Chesapeake Bay is often referred to as the Peninsula.
8. Lieutenant General Robert E. Lee, an Engineer officer in the U.S. Army for many years before the Civil War, commanded the Confederate Army of Northern Virginia from June 1862 to April 1865. Boatner, *Civil War Dictionary*, pp. 476-477.
9. U.S.G. is an abbreviation for Ulysses Simpson Grant.
10. As a second lieutenant of Engineers, Owen received $23.50 a month to hire a servant. He and many other officers hired former slaves as servants. Adjutant General's Office, *Official Register, 1864*, pp. 112-113.

Letter 27
1. Although it is not listed in the index to the *Official Atlas*, Dunkirk, Virginia, does appear on Map 1, Plate 16, southwest of Tappahannock up the Mattapony River from King William Court House.

Letter 28
1. The exact location of Debson's Landing on the James River could not be located.

Letter 29
1. Before the Campaign of 1864 began, the Fiftieth New York Volunteer Engineer Regiment divided into four battalions. The first, second, and third battalions, composed of three companies each, were assigned to the Second, Fifth, and Sixth Army corps, respectively. The reserve battalion consisted of two companies, C and I. Within the reserve battalion, the two ponton trains, Nos. 4 and 5, each had twelve canvas boats and two twin trestles. Captain William Watts Folwell commanded Ponton Train No. 4, and Owen served with it. Paragraph 10, Special Order No. 92, Army of the Potomac, 9 April 1864, Regimental Papers, Fiftieth New York Volunteer Engineer Regiment, MRs 1836-1865, and Reports of Lieutenant Colonel Ira Spaulding, 9, 12, and 20 December 1864, John G. Barnard Papers, General's Papers and Books, RG 94; and *Official Records, Army*, Series I, Volume 36, Part I, pp. 304-316.
2. Early settlers originally built Fort Powhatan, which was located on the banks of the James River near Little Brandon, Virginia. During the Civil War, the Confederates fortified Fort Powhatan but Union troops seized it on 13 July 1863. Porter, *Campaigning with Grant*, p. 49; Heitman, *Historical Register*, p. 535; and *Historical Information Relating to Military Posts and Other Installations ca. 1700*-1900, Microcopy 661 (hereafter referred to as M661), Volume "P," Roll 6, p. 371, RG 94.
3. Windmill Point does not appear in the index to the *Official Atlas* but appears

on Map 1, Plate 92.

4. Brigadier General James Harrison Wilson, a former Topographical Engineer officer, commanded the Third Division, Cavalry Corps, Army of the Potomac, on 30 June 1864. Boatner, *Civil War Dictionary*, pp. 930–931.

5. Mustered in as a captain in Company C on 17 September 1861, Wesley Brainerd received a promotion to major on 28 November 1862 and a brevet lieutenant colonelcy in August 1864. Mustered out of the Fiftieth New York Volunteer Engineer Regiment, he then became the colonel of the Fifteenth New York Volunteer Engineer Regiment. Wesley Brainerd, CMSR, RG 94; and Phisterer, *New York,* pp. 1676–77.

6. Martin Van Brocklin mustered in as first lieutenant of Company I on 18 July 1862. He became captain of Company C on 4 April 1863 and received a brevet lieutenant colonelcy as of 9 April before mustering out of the service on 13 June 1865. Phisterer, *New York*, p. 1687.

Letter 30

1. Light House Point does not appear in the index to the *Official Atlas* but it appears on Map 1, Plate 74. Apparently, Light House Point is the same as Jordans Point.

Letter 31

1. On 9 August 1864, an explosion occurred at City Point, Virginia, on a barge docked at the wharf, which also destroyed a nearby vessel and a building housing large amounts of supplies. Apparently, two Confederate agents, John Maxwell and R.K. Dillard, caused the explosion, which killed and injured many people. *Official Records, Army*, Series I, Volume 42, Part I, pp. 954–956; and Part II, pp. 94–96, 98, 102, and 112.

2. Artificer George Dan died on 21 July 1864 reportedly from "debility aggravated by malingering." Co. I, 50th, DB, RG 94.

3. Rheumatic fever was the cause of artificer James Randall's demise on 30 July 1864. Co. I, 50th, DB, RG 94.

4. On 27 July 1864, artificer Squire A. Kimber died of dysentery. Co. I, 50th, DB, RG 94.

5. Artificer Charley R. Stratton died on 5 August 1864 of peritonitis. Co. I, 50th, DB, RG 94.

Letter 32

1. The Fifth Army Corps served in the Army of the Potomac from May 1862 to June 1865. Major General G.K. Warren commanded it from March 1864 to April 1865. Boatner, *Civil War Dictionary*, pp. 190–191.

2. The Petersburg Railroad was sometimes referred to as the Weldon or Petersburg and Weldon. The line ran from Petersburg, Virginia, to Weldon, North Carolina, with a spur from Hickford, Virginia, to Gaston, North Carolina. Johnston, *Virginia Railroads*, pp. 4 and 6.

Letter 33

1. Petersburg, Virginia.

2. Walker V. Personius mustered in as a captain in Company G on 14 September 1861 and resigned his commission on 20 September 1864. Phisterer, *New York*, p. 1685.

Letter 34
1. Enrolling as a private in Company A at Troy, Pennsylvania, on 11 September 1861, Archibald McNaught received promotions to artificer and sergeant. Given a commission as first lieutenant on 29 April 1864, he became captain of Company H on 6 November and then resigned from the service on 14 January 1865. After leaving the service, McNaught received a brevet majority as of 31 March 1865. Phisterer, *New York*, p. 1683.

Letter 35
1. Under Grant's instructions, the Army constructed a railroad from headquarters at City Point to Globe Tavern at Petersburg, Virginia, during the summer of 1864. In operation by 13 September, this short railroad carried important supplies and material from the wharfs at City Point to the troops at Petersburg. Johnston, *Virginia Railroads*, pp. 220–221.
2. By "Chicago Pill," Owen means the peace plank of the Democratic Party, with which George B. McClellan, the Presidential candidate, did not agree.

Letter 36
1. Most likely, Mr. Warner was the Owen family banker.

Letter 37
1. "Lieutenant Bain" refers to Mahlon Bainbridge Folwell.
2. Apparently, Lincoln won the soldier-in-the-field vote by at least 4 to 1. For information pertaining to the soldier vote and the New York absentee voting process for servicemen, see Peter J. Parish, *The American Civil War* (New York: Holmes and Meier Publisher,. . . Inc., 1975), pp. 543–545. Josiah H. Benton's *Voting in the Field: A Forgotten Chapter of the Civil War* (Boston: Private Printing, 1915) is a lengthy discussion of soldier voting in the Civil War.

Letter 38
1. Lucius A. Waldo, who mustered into Company M as a second lieutenant on 19 February 1864, was cashiered on 18 October 1864. Phisterer, *New York*, p. 1688.
2. Originally mustered in as a private in Company M on 2 January 1864, Edward B. Austin received a commission as first lieutenant on 28 April 1864. He was dismissed from the service on 7 November 1864. Phisterer, *New York*, p. 1675.

Letter 39
1. Private Chauncey Crawford of Company I died of unknown causes on 14 November 1864. Co. I, 50th, DB, RG 94.
2. Charles Hollenbeick, a private in Company I, died on 13 October 1864 of unknown causes. Co. I, 50th, DB, RG 94.

Letter 40
1. Fort Stevenson was a Union redoubt constructed in 1864 for the siege of Petersburg. For the location of Fort Stevenson, see Map 2, Plate 67, and Map 2, Plate 79, in the *Official Atlas*, near Fort Mahan. Volume S, Roll 7, M661, RG 94, p. 594.
2. The term "contraband" was often used during the Civil War to refer to slaves who left their masters and entered Union lines to secure their freedom. The

term originated from some Union commanders who referred to escaped or liberated slaves as "contraband of war." Boatner, *Civil War Dictionary*, p. 172.

Letter 41
1. Poplar Grove or Poplar Grove Church, captured by Union troops on 18–21 August 1864 during the siege of Petersburg, became the camp of the Fiftieth New York Volunteer Engineer Regiment during the winter of 1864–1865. Today, part of the land is the Poplar Grove National Cemetery. For the general location of Poplar Grove Church, see Map 2, Plate 77, in the *Official Atlas*. Richard Wayne Lykes, *Petersburg Battlefields* (Washington, DC: Government Printing Office, 1951), pp. 27 and 52.
2. Also known as the Yellow Tavern, Globe Tavern, Glick House, and Six-Mile House, the Yellow House, a yellow brick structure, was a thriving tavern until the railroads displaced it. For the location of Yellow House (Globe Tavern) on the Petersburg and Weldon Railroad, see Map 8, Plate 67, in the *Official Atlas*. Robert McAllister, *The Civil War Letters of General Robert McAllister*, edited by James I. Robertson (New Brunswick, New Jersey: Rutgers University Press, 1965), p. 533, including fn. 48; Charles S. Wainwright, *A Diary of Battle: The Personal Journal of Colonel Charles S. Wainwright, 1861–1865*, edited by Allan Nevins (New York: Harcourt, Brace and World, Inc., 1862), p. 452; and telephone conversations with historians Ella Reyburn and John Davis of the Petersburg National Military Park and Archivist-Historian Richard Sommers of the U.S. Army Military History Institute, Carlisle Barracks, Pennsylvania.

Letter 43
1. Organized on 22 July 1862, the Ninth Corps served in the Army of the Potomac, Department of the Ohio and Department of Washington. While involved in the siege of Petersburg, Major General John Grubb Parke, a former Topographical Engineer, commanded the corps. Boatner, *Civil War Dictionary*, p. 192.

Letter 44
1. Owen apparently witnessed the hangings for desertion of Privates George Bradley of Company H and John Lynch and William Miller of Company F, Fifth New Hampshire Volunteer Infantry Regiment, on Friday, 23 December 1864. The next Friday, 30 December, a firing squad shot Private Michael Genon, or Jenos, of Company B, Fifth New Hampshire Volunteer Infantry Regiment, for desertion. A week later, on 6 January 1865, Privates Michael West of Company G, 184th Pennsylvania Volunteer Infantry Regiment, and John Benson, unassigned, Fifth New Hampshire Volunteer Infantry Regiment, were shot for desertion. Authorized by Army of the Potomac court martial orders, all of these executions occurred, most likely, in the vicinity of Petersburg, Virginia. However, Owen may have witnessed other executions on 6 January instead of the ones mentioned above. Although the location of the executions is unknown, he may have seen Charles King and Henry Regley of Company L, Third New Jersey Volunteer Cavalry Regiment, shot as spies by order of Philip Sheridan. War Department, *List of U.S. Soldiers Executed by United States Authorities During the Late War* (Washington, DC: War Department Printing Office, n.d.)
2. Engineer troops built numerous towers, varying from very crude to sophisticated structures, from which the U.S. Signal Corps could send messages

by the use of flags and be seen for long distances. For a drawing and photograph of signal towers constructed by Engineers, see No. 10, Plate 67, and No. 9, Plate 124, in the *Official Atlas*.

3. Benjamin F. Butler led an unsuccessful expedition against Fort Fisher, North Carolina, in November 1864. On 4 January 1865, troops under the command of Alfred H. Terry left Bermuda Hundreds on a second attempt to capture Fort Fisher and seal off the port of Wilmington, North Carolina, to foreign trade. The fort surrendered on 15 January. Boatner, *Civil War Dictionary*, pp. 292-295.

4. In January 1864, Owen was on leave in Owego. Most likely, while on leave Owen heard Edward Norris Kirk, a prominent Presbyterian and Congregationalist minister and revivalist, speak in Owego or some neighboring town. During the Civil War, Kirk, a strong advocate of the Union cause, held many revivals in the East. Johnson and Malone, *DAB*, Volume 5, pp. 427-428.

Letter 45

1. During the winter of 1864-1865, while encamped at Poplar Grove, the Fiftieth New York Volunteer Engineer Regiment constructed quarters and other buildings including a church of hewn logs. W.J. George, "Church Built, at Petersburg, by Engineers During Civil War," *Professional Memoirs, Corps of Engineers* 4 (July-August 1912), pp. 521-522.

2. Owen here refers to the capture by the Union troops of Fort Fisher, a casemated earthwork constructed by the Confederates on the right bank of the Cape Fear River at Federal Point, approximately 20 miles below Wilmington, North Carolina. Although, Union troops did not occupy Wilmington until 22 February 1865, the blockade runner traffic, an important economy of the city and the Confederacy, all but ceased after the capture of the Cape Fear defenses. Volume F, Roll 3, M661, RG 94, p. 151; Boatner, *Civil War Dictionary*, pp. 293-294; and Dallas Irvine, John Ferrell, Dale Floyd, Robert Gruber, and Francis Heppner, *Military Operations of the Civil War: A Guide-Index to the Official Records of the Union and Confederate Armies, 1861-1865* (Washington, DC: Government Printing Office, 1968-1980), Volume 2, Fascicle 2, p. 105, and Volume 3, p. 45.

3. Lincoln appointed Benjamin F. Butler a general in 1861 because of his political influence as a Democrat and lawyer. After holding various commands, Butler led the unsuccessful attack on Fort Fisher, North Carolina, during 7-27 December 1864. On 7 January 1865, Lincoln and Grant relieved Butler of his command of the Army of the James. He returned to his home in Lowell, Massachusetts, an industrial center, which manufactured shoes among other things. Boatner, *Civil War Dictionary*, pp. 292-293, and Johnson and Malone, *DAB*, Volume 2, pp. 357-359.

Letter 46

1. Because Confederate batteries and Union obstructions kept federal gunboats from proceeding up the James River, Benjamin F. Butler suggested a bypass canal. Captain Peter S. Michie, an Engineer officer, began construction of the Dutch Gap Canal on 10 August 1864, but it was not completed until April 1865, too late to be of use to the Union war effort. Boatner, *Civil War Dictionary*, p. 253.

2. On the evening of 23 January 1865, a Confederate fleet attempted to pass the obstructions in the James River and head upriver toward Richmond. Union artillery fired on it during the night of the 23d and morning of the 24th. Finally,

the fleet retreated downriver leaving one ship aground. On the 25th, the fleet successfully ran past the Union guns and proceeded upriver. *Official Records, Army*, Series I, Volume 46, Part I, pp. 165–170, 176–179, 181–182, and 186.
3. During the Civil War, numerous Union officers received temporary or honorary brevet rank, usually for meritorious service or actions. Thus, a captain could be a brevet brigadier general and might function at one or the other rank depending on his assignment. Following the war, officers normally reverted to their permanent rank but could sign official documents and wear insignia denoting brevet under certain conditions. For more information on brevet rank, see Don Russell's introduction to Percival Lowe's *Five Years a Dragon* (Reprint, Norman, Oklahoma: University of Oklahoma Press, 1965).
4. "General P.H.S." refers to Philip H. Sheridan.
5. The Quartermaster's Department chartered the 531-ton steamer *Thomas Colyer*, owned by George B. Colyer, for $240.18 per day from 1 November 1864 to 5 May 1865. The Army of the Valley, officially the Army of the Shenandoah, Middle Military Division, was established by Sheridan in August 1864. Sheridan held command of the Army of the Shenandoah until February 1865, when Major General Alfred Torbet took over followed by Major General Winfield Scott Hancock in March. "Collyer, Thomas," Charters, Bills of Lading, Claims Papers, Plans and Correspondence Relating to Vessels ("Vessel File"), 1834–1900, RG 92; Congress, *House Executive Document No. 337, Vessels Bought, Sold, and Chartered by the United States, 1861–68* (40th Cong., 2d sess.), pp. 22–23; and Boatner, *Civil War Dictionary*, pp. 549 and 739.

Letter 47
1. The South Side Railroad had 132 miles of track stretching from City Point to Lynchburg, Virginia. Johnston, *Virginia Railroads*, pp. 4 and 6.

Letter 48
1. In 1865, the federal government purchased "The Battle of Lake Erie," painted by William H. Powell under contract. It now hangs in the Senate wing of the Capitol in the east staircase. Architect of the Capitol, *Compilation of Works*, pp. 126–130.
2. Noah Brooks, newspaper correspondent who spent most of the Civil War in Washington, D.C., wrote that a full-length, life-size portrait of Grant, painted in oil by John Antrobus of Chicago, hung in one of the committee rooms of the House of Representatives on 29 February 1864. Possibly, this painting later hung in the rotunda. Noah Brooks, *Mr. Lincoln's Washington: The Civil War Dispatches of Noah Brooks*, edited by P.J. Staudenraus (New York: Thomas Yoseloff, 1967), pp. 288–289.
3. The Quartermaster's Department completed work on the outside of the Capitol dome on 2 December 1863 but, of course, the inside took longer. On 25 November 1864, Noah Brooks remarked that the interior of the dome was just completed. Albert E. Cowdrey, *A City for the Nation: The Army Engineers and the Building of Washington, D.C., 1790–1967* (Washington, DC: Government Printing Office, 1979), p. 21; and Brooks, *Mr. Lincoln's Washington*, p. 391.

Letter 49
1. The pike went from Winchester to Staunton, Virginia.
2. George Armstrong Custer graduated from the U.S. Military Academy in 1861 and as a cavalry commander he became a major general of volunteers on

15 April 1865 when only 25 years of age. Custer commanded the Third Cavalry Division in the Shenandoah. He is best known for his disastrous defeat and death at the Battle of the Little Big Horn in 1876. Boatner, *Civil War Dictionary*, p. 216.

3. Resigning his cadetship at West Point in May 1861, Thomas Lafayette Rosser became an officer in the Confederate army. As a brigadier general, commissioned in September 1863, he led a cavalry brigade in the Shenandoah Valley and met Custer in battle several times. Boatner, *Civil War Dictionary*, pp. 709–710.

4. Jubal A. Early, a graduate of the U.S. Military Academy who had served in the U.S. Regular Army, joined the Confederate forces in 1861. Rising to major general, he commanded an army corps in Lee's Army of Northern Virginia. In June 1864, he took his corps to the Shenandoah Valley where he encountered Sheridan's troops numerous times. Boatner, *Civil War Dictionary*, pp. 224–225.

5. In 1832, the James River and Kanawha Company, formed from the James River Company, initiated plans for a James River and Kanawha Canal. Construction ended in 1851 with the canal completed from Richmond to Buchanan, Virginia. Owen returned from the Shenandoah Valley to the Petersburg area by traversing the towpath of the James River and Kanawha Canal. *Official Records, Army*, Series I, Volume 46, Part I, pp. 488–495; and Johnson and Malone, *DAB*, Volume 3, p. 488. *See also* Wayland F. Dunaway, *History of the James River and Kanawha Company* (New York: Columbia University Press, 1922); and James J. Kirkwood, *Waterways to the West, James River and Kanawha* (Washington, DC: Eastern National Parks and Monument Association, 1936).

6. The Virginia Central Railroad ran 195 miles from Richmond to Jackson's River, Virginia. Johnston, *Virginia Railroads*, pp. 4–5.

Letter 50

1. On Thursday and Friday, 16 and 17 March 1865, Owego Creek overflowed and caused a record flood in Owego, New York. In fact, the large Susquehanna River and its many tributaries caused record floods throughout New York and Pennsylvania in the spring of 1865. *The Owego Gazette*, 23 and 30 March 1865.

2. Unfortunately, the location of Five Mile Creek could not be found on the various maps available but, most likely, a more specific one might show the stream.

3. Established in 1864, the Army of the James was commanded by Benjamin F. Butler. Intended to threaten Richmond from the south and east while Grant descended on the city from the north, Butler's command failed miserably. Confederate forces maneuvered the Army of the James into Bermuda Hundreds, where it remained until late in the war. *Dictionary of American History*, Volume 3, p. 488.

4. Presumably, Hancock Station was a depot on Grant's City Point and Petersburg Railroad. The exact location of Hancock Station, probably named for Winfield Scott Hancock, is unknown.

5. In his report dated 16 May 1865, Philip H. Sheridan, commander of cavalry in the Army of the Potomac, stated ". . . I moved out on the 29th March, in conjunction with the armies operating against Richmond. . . ." The 29th was the starting date of the Appomattox Campaign, 29 March–9 April 1865. *Official Records, Army*, Series I, Volume 46, Part I, pp. 557 and 1101–10.

Letter 51
1. The Confederates established a battery at Howlett's House in June 1864 to fire upon Union ships attempting to pass up the James River. Also known as Battery Dantzler, the Howlett House Battery was located on the James River at Trent's Reach across from Farrar's Island. For the exact location of the battery, see Map 3, Plate 77, in the *Official Atlas* and the map between pages 632 and 633 in Volume 11, Series I, of Navy Department, *Official Records of the Union and Confederate Navies in the War of the Rebellion* (Washington, DC: Government Printing Office, 1894–1922) (hereafter referred to as *Official Records, Navy*). *Official Records, Army*, Series I, Volume 40, Part II, pp. 290 and 302; and *Official Records, Navy*, Series I, Volume 10, pp. 185, 666, 709, and 730. See also next annotation.
2. Battery Dantzler, Howlett House Battery, mounted different numbers of guns, including Brookes and Columbiads, at various times. The Brooke, developed by John M. Brooke of the Confederate Navy, was a cast-iron gun, usually rifled, and easily identifiable by its reinforced hooped rings. The Columbiad, developed before the War of 1812, was a large-caliber, usually smoothbore cannon able to fire heavy charged shot and shell at high elevations. Edward S. Farrow, *Farrow's Military Encyclopedia: A Dictionary of Military Knowledge; Illustrated with Maps and About Three Thousand Wood Engravings* (New York: Edward S. Farrow, 1885), Volume I, p. 249; Boatner, *Civil War Dictionary*, pp. 88 and 167–168; Emanuel Raymond Lewis, "The Ambiguous Columbiads," *Military Affairs* 28 (Fall 1964), pp. 111–112; Warren Ripley, *Artillery and Ammunition of the Civil War* (New York: Van Nostrand Reinhold Company, 1970), pp. 127–128; *Official Records, Army*, Series I, Volume 42, Part II, p. 1222, and Part III, p. 1354; *Official Records, Navy*, Series I, Volume 10, pp. 698, 709, and 738–739, and Volume 11, p. 206; and Henry L. Abbot, *Siege Artillery in the Campaign Against Richmond*, Professional Papers, Corps of Engineers, No. 14 (Washington, DC: Government Printing Office, 1867), p. 121. For pictures of guns mounted at Battery Dantzler, see Francis T. Miller, *The Photographic History of the Civil War* (New York: The Review of Reviews Company, 1911), Volume 3, pp. 93 and 97. Various photographs of Brookes and Columbiads can be found in Ripley, *Artillery and Ammunition*.
3. During the Civil War, a gun was "spiked" by forcing a spike into the vent of the gun and breaking it off, thus rendering the gun inoperable. Quick, *Dictionary of Weapons*, p. 415.
4. In a report dated 4 April 1865, Admiral David Dixon Porter stated that the Confederates had sunk their ships in the James River and some of them were in sight above the water. Apparently, Owen saw one of these sunken ships on 4 April 1865. *Official Records, Navy*, Series I, Volume 12, p. 101.
5. Jefferson ("Jeff") Davis, the president of the Confederate States of America, was a graduate of the U.S. Military Academy, and former Regular Army officer, Secretary of War, and senator from Mississippi. Many southerners held Davis personally responsible for Confederate defeat. Boatner, *Civil War Dictionary*, pp. 225–226.
6. Alexander Piper, formerly a Regular Army artillery officer, served as colonel of the Tenth New York Heavy Artillery Regiment. Mustered into service in September 1862 at Sackett's Harbor, New York, the Tenth served in the Defenses of Washington, Army of the Potomac, Army of the James, and Middle Military Department. The regiment mustered out of the service at Petersburg, Virginia, on 23 June 1865. Phisterer, *New York*, p. 1455; and Dyer, *A Com-*

pendium, Volume 3, p. 1386.

Letter 53
1. Although attacked, William Henry Seward, Secretary of State, did not die from his injuries. Boatner, *Civil War Dictionary*, p. 732.
2. "Mr. Johnson," refers to Andrew Johnson, who had been Vice President under Lincoln and succeeded to the Presidency following the assassination.

Letter 54
1. The insignia for colonels in the U.S. Army since before the Civil War is a spread eagle. Thus Owen referred to the colonels by calling them "spread eagles," *Uniform Regulations for the Army of the United States 1861* (Washington, DC: Smithsonian Institution, 1961), p. 18.
2. Most likely, Owen's reference to "nigger show" denoted minstrel shows. During the winter of 1864–1865, the Fiftieth New York Volunteer Engineer Regiment held minstrel shows almost every night in the church at Poplar Grove. Apparently, Owen felt that all the high-ranking officials cared about were minstrel shows and they were not concerned with military matters. George, "Church Built," p. 521.
3. Joseph E. Johnston, a former Topographical Engineer officer, commanding the Confederate Army of Tennessee, wrote William T. Sherman, commanding the Military Division of the Mississippi, on 14 April 1865 to initiate peace negotiations. On 18 April, Johnston and Sherman signed an accord which authorities in Washington rejected. The final surrender occurred at Durham Station, North Carolina, on 26 April. *Official Records, Army*, Series I, Volume 47, Part I, pp. 31–35 and 937–938.

Letter 55
1. Established on 7 August 1864, the Middle Military Division included all or part of the states of Pennsylvania, Delaware, West Virginia, Ohio, Maryland, and Virginia. The War Department discontinued the Middle Military Division on 27 June 1865. Raphael P. Thian, compiler, *Notes Illustrating the Military Geography of the United States 1813-1880* (Reprint, Austin: University of Texas Press, 1979), p. 21.
2. Mustered into the service as a private in Company G on 20 August 1862, Mahlon Bainbridge received promotions to corporal and sergeant. When Owen became a first lieutenant as of 15 October 1864, Bainbridge transferred to Company I to fill the vacancy. Commissioned a second lieutenant in Company I on 23 January 1865, Bainbridge served in that capacity until mustered out on 13 June 1865. Phisterer, *New York*, pp. 1675–76.
3. "Sherman's Blunder" refers to that general's failure to negotiate a surrender of Joseph Johnston's forces on 18 April 1865 that was acceptable to authorities in Washington.
4. Owen means Stephenson's Depot or Station on the Winchester and Potomac Railroad just above Winchester. For the exact location of Stephenson's Depot or Station, see Map 4, Plate 39, and Map 3, Plate 43, in the *Official Atlas*.
5. M. Truman Smyth mustered into the service as a private in Company I on August 1862. Promoted to artificer on 1 April 1864, he later served as a clerk. Smyth mustered out of the service on 13 June 1865. M. Truman Smyth, CMSR, RG 94.

Engineer ponton train on the move, from *Frank Leslie's Illustrated*, January 3, 1863.

Thomas Owen's Diary
29 April–18 May 1864

April 29th 1864 Friday
Orders to march. Left winter camp[1] at 7½ A.M. Moved canvas pontons to Kelly's Ford, where we bridged the Rappahannock for Gregg's division of cavalry to cross on. Finished building at 1½ P.M. Cavalry crossed in the afternoon. Moved companies over on the west side of the river. Lay down for the night.

April 30th 1864 Saturday[2]
Turned out at daylight and took up bridge. Took breakfast. Loaded wagons and moved to Paoli Mills[3] and camped. Put up tents. All done about noon. Received orders to report to winter camp for muster. Started on foot after dinner for the old camp. Arrived there and was mustered as second lieutenant at 4½ P.M. Stayed in old tent all night.

May 1st 1864 Sunday
Came back from old camp this morning. Company lay in camp all day.

May 2nd 1864 Monday
Lay in camp today. At work on payrolls, clothing rolls, etc. Heavy squall came up at 5 P.M. Heavy winds, plenty of dust, until the rain began to fall, and then we had a soaking in our thin shelter tent.

May 3rd 1864 Tuesday
Moved at 7 A.M. with train to Richardsville[4] and camped about noon in pine woods. Worked on clothing rolls in afternoon. Fine weather.

May 4th 1864 Wednesday
Broke camp at 11 P.M last night and took the road to Ely's Ford. On the road until daylight when we arrived at the ford and immediately commenced laying bridge, which we finished in an hour and a half. Gregg's cavalry forded the river before we laid the bridge. As soon as we finish[ed], the 2d Corps commenced crossing. Took breakfast at 9¼. Commenced taking up bridge and, in our train, started for Chancellorsville, where we arrived at 2½ P.M. and stopped for the night.

May 5th 1864 Thursday
March this A.M. at 7 A.M. towards the front. Passed the Leak House.[5] Followed a train all day that moved very slow. Towards night received orders to rightabout and at dark were at Chancellorsville.

May 6th 1864 Friday
Received orders last night to report to the front at daylight. At 10 P.M. started with 3 days' rations in hav[er]sacks but unfortunate for the commissary, the wagon contain[ing] mess chest was left to____. At daylight, went into the rifle pits just to the left of the Plank Road where our men had ____ from just before. Lay in pits until about noon. Then went to work throwing up traverse.[6] Then [in] rifle pits until night. Went back to pits and soon ordered to the right to fill pits in rear of [New] Jersey Brigade which had broke[n].[7]

May 7th 1864 [Saturday]
Lay in rifle pits all night. We moved at about 10½ A.M. thinking the enemy coming. About dark last night, the [New] Jersey Brigade of the +[8] broke and came in over the pits, where they again rallied. Just after daylight were relieved from the pits and went just in rear of General Warren['s] headquarters, where we lay until sundown. Then started for Chancellorsville.

May 8th 1864 Sunday
Arrived at Chancellorsville about midnight. Lay down near the remains of the old tavern[9] until 4 A.M. when were called up. Took breakfast. The rest of the companies left us here. Company C came up with canvas train and we started on the Fredericksburg Pike towards that place. Turned to the right on the Mine Road to the Plank. Then to the left down Plank to Spotsylvania Road. Followed that several miles. Turned back very quick. Came back to the Plank and towards Chancellorsville as far as the Mine Road. Lay there until dark and started up the Plank.[10] Then turned to the left and went over the Ny River to Piney Branch Church, where we arrived just before day. Lay down until morning. Wounded went to Fredericksburg.

May 9th 1864 Monday
Lay by the roadside all day in pine grove. A good rest. Fighting heavy.

May 10th 1864 Sunday
Lay in camp today. Company C went with their train to Po River and bridged it. Heavy firing to the left of us. News today that Butler

is in Petersburg and advancing on Richmond.[11] Sherman is driving the enemy.[12] At sundown, fell in with arms, etc. Moved train in the [   ] which is full of supply and ammunition _____.

May 11th 1864 Wednesday
Was rear guard for all the trains on this road last night. Came to the Plank where we found the train about 1 A.M. and lay down for the night. Lay around all day. Rather warm fight continues. Towards night heavy shower. I was sent out on picket with 40 men from each company at dusk. Remained until 10½ P.M. and returned to camp wet through.

May 12th 1864 Thursday
Firing commenced before light this morning. Heavy cannonading all day. Some rain. The fight is southeast of us and southwest of Fredericksburg. We lay with the reserve artillery. Towards night received orders to move from Bensons to Zoan Church on the Fredericksburg Pike.

May 13th 1864 Friday
Was on the road all night, it being blocked up with trains ahead. A little after daylight went into camp near Zoan Church. Lay still all day. Slept. Some reports says we have taken Richmond. No fighting today. Enemy reported gone. Still continues wet. Teams went yesterday to Belle Plain after forage. Roads bad.

May 14th 1864 Saturday
Cloudy. Order from General Meade stating we have taken, in the late fight, 8,000 prisoners, 22 stands colors, 18 pieces artillery. Broke camp about 8 A.M. Moved below Salem Church, a distance of two or three miles. Saw Colonel Tracey[13] of the 109th [New York, Volunteer Infantry Regiment] in the afternoon. Likewise viewed others of that regiment. Pleasant shower towards night.

May 15th 1864 Sunday
Broke camp at 10 A.M. Moved to Fredericksburg. Camped just south of Marye's Heights.[14] Enemy reported in our rear. Trains all moving to this city. Went down to the river at night and got some fish of Company G, they being in charge of the bridge at the lower part of the city. Fredericksburg presents a pleasing sight from the surrounding hills.

May 16th 1864 Monday
Lay in camp at Fredericksburg all day. Little going on of interest. A depot of supplies is open at Belle Plain and the Army is now getting forage and rations from the place. Colonel Schriver[15] is

military governor of Fredericksburg. General Benham is at Belle Plain with a detachment of the 15th New York. Major Ford[16] was here today. Just came from Washington.

May 17th 1864 Tuesday
Breakfast at 5 A.M. Orders to move to the front. Broke camp early and marched to General Meade's headquarters near Anderson House close to the Ny River.[17] Reserve Artillery attached to corps and sent to the front.

May 18th 1864 Wednesday
Broke camp very early and moved 2 miles towards the right of our line. Quite a stir among hospitals, etc. Some sharp fighting in the early part of the day. Company built corduroy bridge over swamp and came back to same camp we left this morning. All hospitals, etc., go back to same camp.

NOTES TO DIARY

1. Rappahannock Station, Virginia.

2. For operations of the Fiftieth New York Volunteer Engineer Regiment and Company I at the battles of the Wilderness and Spotsylvania Court House, see pages 303-316 in Part I, Volume 36, Series I, of War Department, *The War of the Rebellion: A Compilation of the Official Records of the Union and Confederate Armies* (Washington, DC: Government Printing Office, 1880-1901) (hereafter referred to as *Official Records, Army*).

3. Paoli Mills is southwest of Kelly's Ford on Map 3, Plate 44, in War Department, *Atlas to Accompany the Official Records of the Union and Confederate Armies* (Washington, DC: Government Printing Office, 1891-1895) (hereafter referred to as *Official Atlas*).

4. Richardsville, Virginia, which is southwest of Ellis Ford, can also be found on the map cited in the annotation above.

5. The Leak House could not be located on the various maps consulted.

6. A traverse is a wall of dirt erected to safeguard men in a rifle pit from enfilading fire. Henry L. Scott, *Military Dictionary* (New York: D. Van Nostrand, 1861), p. 625; Philip Babcock Grove, editor in chief, *Webster's Third New International Dictionary of the English Language Unabridged* (Springfield, Massachusetts: G. and C. Merriam Company, Publishers, 1961), p. 2433; and Robert I. Alotta, *A Glossary of Fortification Terms as They Relate to Historic Old Fort Mifflin* (Philadelphia: The Shackamaxon Society, Inc., 1972).

7. Lieutenant Colonel Ira Spaulding reported that on 6 May 1864 "just before dark...the enemy succeeded in flanking and breaking a division of the Sixth Corps on our front and right and drove them behind the second line" of rifle pits. Confederate General Jubal A. Early's men attacked Horatio G. Wright's First Division of the Sixth Corps on its rear and flank. One brigade, commanded by Alexander Shaler, sustained the brunt of the attack with the loss of many men killed, wounded, and captured. The attack and resulting confusion caused panic within the other brigades of the division and generally throughout the Sixth Corps. The First Brigade of Wright's Division, commanded by Colonel Henry W. Brown, comprised the First, Second, Third, Fourth, Tenth, and Fifteenth New Jersey volunteer infantry regiments. Apparently, some soldiers from this New Jersey Brigade panicked and ran pell-mell back to the rifle pits occupied by Owen and his men. Officers of the Sixth Corps rallied their men, the Confederates quit the attack, and darkness ended the conflict. *Official Records, Army*, Series I, Volume 36, Part I, pp. 11 and 307; J.H. Stine, *History of the Army of the Potomac: The Wilderness Campaign* (Harrisburg, Pennsylvania: The Stackpole Company, 1960), pp. 440-450; Camille Baquet, *History of the First Brigade, New Jersey Volunteers from 1861 to 1865* (Trenton, New Jersey: MacCrellish and Quigley, State Printers, 1910), pp. 116-118; and Alanson A. Haines, *The History of the Fifteenth Regiment, New Jersey Volunteers* (New York: Jenkins and Thomas, Printers, 1883), pp. 146-153.

8. During the Civil War, the various Union Army Corps adopted designating symbols which were sewn or attached to their headgear. The New Jersey Brigade belonged to the Sixth Corps, whose first symbol or corps badge was the St. Andrew's Cross. Later, the corps switched its badge to the George's Cross. Thus, Owen's inclusion of + is a reference to the Sixth Corps. John D. Billings, *Hardtack and Coffee or the Unwritten Story of Army Life* (Boston: George M. Smith and Company, 1887), pp. 254-268.

9. Most likely, Owen slept near the remains of the Chancellor House at Chancellorsville. The headquarters of Joseph Hooker during the Battle of Chancellorsville, the Chancellor House later burned. Joseph P. Cullen, *Where a Hundred Thousand Fell: The Battles of Fredericksburg, Chancellorsville, the Wilderness and Spotsylvania Court House* (Washington, DC: Government Printing Office, 1966), p. 29.

10. For an understanding of the road network in the Wilderness-Spotsylvania area, see *Official Atlas*, especially Map 1, Plate 41; Map 3, Plate 55; Map 1, Plate 81; Map 1, Plate 91; and Map 1, Plate 96. *See also* Cullen, *Where a Hundred Thousand Fell*.

11. When the 1864 Union campaign began, Major Benjamin F. Butler, Commander of the Army of the James, began to move north and threaten Richmond and its communications with the southern states. Experiencing some initial success including the seizure of City Point, Virginia, Butler allowed his army to be bottled up at Bermuda Hundreds on the south side of the James River by a smaller Confederate force on 17 May 1864. Richard W. Lykes, *Petersburg Battlefields* (Washington, DC: Government Printing Office, 1951), pp. 2-3; and Mark M. Boatner, *The Civil War Dictionary* (New York: David McKay Company, Inc., 1959), p. 61.

12. In early May of 1864, William T. Sherman's troops began an advance on the Confederate forces opposing him in the West. Sherman's movements resulted in the capture of Atlanta, Georgia, in September 1864. Boatner, *Civil War Dictionary*, p. 30.

13. Benjamin Franklin Tracey was colonel and commander of the 109th New York Volunteer Infantry Regiment from 28 August 1862-17 May 1864 and received a Congressional Medal of Honor for his service at the Battle of the Wilderness. His regiment organized at Binghamton, New York, and mustered into federal service on 27 August 1862. Serving with the Middle Department and Department of Washington before joining the Army of the Potomac, it fought in numerous battles before mustering out on 4 June 1865. Possibly, Owen knew Colonel Tracey from New York or from association with him in the Army. Also, since Binghamton is not far from Owego, some of Owen's friends and neighbors may have enlisted in the regiment. Boatner, *Civil War Dictionary*, p. 845; and Frederick B. Dyer, *A Compendium of the War of the Rebellion* (Reprint, New York: Thomas Yoseloff, Publisher, 1959), Volume 3, p. 1448.

14. Marye's Heights is a ridge behind Fredericksburg, Virginia. In the Battle of Fredericksburg, 13 December 1862, hundreds of Union soldiers marched up Marye's Heights and forfeited their lives in an unsuccessful attempt to dislodge

Confederate forces from a virtually impregnable position at the top of the ridge. Cullen, *Where a Hundred Thousand Fell*, pp. 14–15 and 21.

15. Edmund Schriver, a graduate of the U.S. Military Academy in 1833 and a Regular Army officer from 1833 until he resigned in 1846, received a commission as lieutenant colonel in the Eleventh U.S. Infantry at the beginning of the Civil War. During the war he served in various staff positions. He was commanding officer at Fredericksburg for some time and part of his correspondence appears in the *Official Records, Army*, especially Series I, Volume 36, Part II. After the war, Schriver remained in the Army and served as Inspector General twice before resigning in 1881. Dumas Malone, editor, *Dictionary of American Biography* (New York: Charles Scribner's Sons, 1935), Volume 8, p. 463.

16. Formerly serving as first sergeant in the Seventh New York State Militia at the beginning of the Civil War, George W. Ford mustered in as a captain in Company A of the Fiftieth New York Volunteer Engineer Regiment on 18 September 1861. Promoted to major on 9 April 1864, Ford resigned from the service on 25 March 1865 after receiving a brevet lieutenant colonelcy of volunteers dating from 1 August 1864. Frederick Phisterer, compiler, *New York in the War of the Rebellion 1861 to 1865* (Albany: J.B. Lyon Company, 1912), p. 1679.

17. The "Anderson House" referred to by Owen was a farmhouse located about a mile and a half east and a little north of Spotsylvania Court House near the Ny River. Robert McAllister, *The Civil War Letters of General Robert McAllister*, edited by James I. Robertson (New Brunswick, New Jersey: Rutgers University Press, 1965), p. 424, fn. 23, and *Official Atlas*, Plate 55, Map 2.

INDEX TO LETTERS

(This index covers the Owen letters only, not the introduction and diary, which are short enough to require none. All references refer to letter numbers, not page numbers.)

Albany, NY: 19
Albert, Owen's servant: 26, 39, 40
Alexandria, VA: 1, 15
Annapolis, MD: 46
Armstrong, John E.: 6
Army of the James: 50
Army of the Potomac: 6, 35, 50
Artillery: 2, 6, 19, 20, 51
Austin, Edward B.: 38
Axes: 2

Bacon, Francis: 24
Bainbridge, Mahlon: 55
Balls Crossroads, VA: 11
Barricade, brush: 20
Batteries, artillery: 19, 20, 51
Bealton, VA: 11, 13
Beers, Albert B.: 18
Belle Plain, VA: 25
Benham, George W.: 5
Bensen's Farm: 25
Berlin, MD: 8
Bermuda Hundreds, VA: 46
Berry, J.: 18
Bodle, Charles R.: 24
Booth, John Wilkes: 53
Bowling Green, VA: 26, 27
Brainerd, Wesley: 29
Brandy Station, VA: 15
Bridges: 6, 8, 11, 25, 26, 28, 43, 49, 50; wooden, 26; wooden ponton, 26; corduroy, 26
Bridging operations: 5, 6, 8, 11, 25, 26, 28, 30, 43, 49, 50; corduroy, 26; *see also* pontons
Bristoe Station, VA: 11
Brooke gun: 51
Bull Run Creek, VA: 1, 11
Bunzey, John H.: 15, 24
Burkeville, VA: 54
Burnside, Ambrose E.: 4
Butler, Benjamin F.: 45

Camp organization: buildings, 13, 43, 45; church, 45; dress parade, 20; drill, 18, 20; erecting tents for new recruits, 19; guard mountings, 20; inspection, 15; muster day, 34; posting pickets, 33; ponton park, 50; routine, 16
Camps: *see under name of camp*
Capitol, Washington, DC: 11, 24, 48
Casparis Hotel, Washington, DC: 24
Catlet's Station, VA: 11
Cavalry Corps, Army of the Potomac: 28, 29, 30, 31, 50

Centreville, VA: 11
Champlin, Hanson G.: 5
Champlin, Lester G.: 18, 37, 54
Chancellorsville, VA: 25
Chaplain: 15
Charles City Court House, VA: 2, 29
Charleston, SC: 10
Charlottesville, VA: 49
Chesterfield, VA: 26, 49
Chickahominy Creek, VA: 2, 26, 50
City Point, VA: 29, 30, 31, 32, 33, 34, 35, 36, 37, 38, 39, 40, 42, 43, 46, 50, 51, 52, 53, 54, 55
Columbia, VA: 49
Columbiads: 51
Combat engineering: *see* Military engineering, Bridging operations, Roads, Forts and fortifications
Combat operations: posted in rifle pits, 33; in line of battle, 25; *see also* Bridging operations, Roads, Forts and fortification
Conscripts: 9
Copperheads: 35
Corduroy bridge: 26
Corduroy roads: 35
Court marshal: 24
Crawford, Chauncey: 39
Culpeper, VA: 14, 15
Culpeper County, VA: 15
Custer, George A.: 49

Dan, George: 31
Davis, Jefferson: 51
Debson's Landing, VA: 28
Draft: 8, 13, 35
Dunkirk, VA: 27
Dutch Gap, VA: 46, 51

Early, Jubal A.: 49
Edwards Ferry, MD: 7
Election, 1864: 35, 37, 39
Eleventh Corps: 11
Elmira, NY: 8
Ely: 7
Ely's Ford, VA: 25
Engineer Depot: *see* Volunteer Engineer Depot
Episcopal Church (Trinity), Washington, DC: 24
Equipment: 2, 47; *see also* pontons
Erie Railway: 12
Executions: 44

Fairfax, VA: 11
Fairfax Station, VA: 11
Falmouth, VA: 3, 5, 6
Ferguson, Jefferson: 18, 55
Fifth Corps: 32, 34, 35, 42, 43
First Corps: 14
Fisher, Fort, NC: 45
Five Mile Creek, VA: 50

Flood: 50, 54, 55
Folwell, Mahlon Bainbridge: 23, 31, 37, 46
Folwell, William Watts: 6, 13, 23, 24, 29, 31, 35, 46
Foraging: 26
Ford's Theatre, Washington, DC: 53
Forsyth, George: 10, 16
Forts: *see under name of fort*
Forts and fortifications: 34, 35, 36, 44; brush barricade around artillery emplacements, 20; constructing batteries, 19; stockade, 23; throwing up rifle pits, 25
Frank Leslie's Illustrated: 2
Frear, John: 12
Frederick City, MD: 7
Fredericksburg, VA: 5, 6, 25, 26
Fredericksburg and Richmond Railroad: 26
Fridley, Aaron: 22

Georgetown, Washington, DC: 8
Goodrich, Philip R.: 4
Gordonsville, VA: 15, 27
Grant, Ulysses Simpson (U.S.G.): 20, 26, 28, 32, 48, 50, 52; painting of, 48
Green Point, NY: 39
Gregg, David McMurtie: 25, 29

Hancock, Winfield Scott: 26, 55
Hancock Station, VA: 50
Hanovertown, VA: 26
Harpers Ferry, WV: 7, 55
Harrison's Landing, VA: 2, 50
Hazel Run, VA: 24
Hollenbeick, Charles: 39
Hooker, Joseph: 4, 5, 6
Howlett House Battery, VA: 51
Hunt, Frederick: 18
Huntley's Crossing, VA: 26

Inspection: 15

Jacksonville, NY: 31
James River, VA: 2, 28, 29, 30, 49, 50, 51
Johnson, Andrew: 53
Johnston, Joseph E.: 54
Johnsville, MD: 7

Kanawha Canal: 49
Kelly's Ford, VA: 25
Kimber, Squire A.: 31
King and Queen Court House, VA: 27
Kipp, William H.: 22
Kirk, Edward: 44

LaGrange, Caleb: 24
LaGrange, Henry: 8, 17, 32
Lee, Robert E.: 26, 35, 51, 54, 55
Lesley, Camp, Washington, DC: *see* Volunteer Engineer Depot
Liberty (Libertytown), MD: 7
Light House Point, VA: 30, 31

Lincoln, Abraham: 35, 38, 51, 53
"Little Mac": 4; *see also* McClellan, George B.
Long Bridge, VA: 11
Louisa Court House, VA: 49
Lowell, MA: 45
Lucretia: 10

Manassas, VA: 1, 11
Manassas Junction, VA: 1
Marches: 1, 7, 11, 14, 15, 25, 26, 27, 28, 29, 31, 40, 43, 46, 47, 49, 50, 54
Marshall, George: 24
Mattaponi River, VA: 26, 27
McClellan, George B.: 26, 35; *see also* "Little Mac"
McNaught, Archibald: 34
Meade, George G.: 13, 15, 25, 26
Milford, VA: 26
Milicent, (Owen?): 19, 23, 39, 44
Military engineering: destroying railroads, 49; *see also* Bridging operations, Forts and fortifications, Roads
Monroe, Fort (Fortress), VA: 1
Mortars: 2, 51
Mount Crawford, VA: 49
Mount Jackson, VA: 49
Murphy, J. McLeod: 1
Muster day: 34

New Castle, VA: 27
New Market, VA: 7, 49
New York (Empire State): 10, 22, 23
New York City: 39
New York regiments: 15th Volunteer Engineer Regiment, 1, 24; 10th Volunteer Heavy Artillery Regiment, 51; 5th Volunteer Cavalry Regiment, 26; 3d Volunteer Infantry Regiment, 12; 137th Volunteer Infantry Regiment, 11
Newcome, Calvin Q.: 6
Newell, Orvin L.: 24
Newton, John: 14
9th Corps: 43
North Anna River, VA: 26
Nottoway River, VA: 43
Ny River, VA: 25, 26

"Old Grounds," Washington, DC: *see* Volunteer Engineer Depot
Owego, NY: 10, 11, 12, 17, 24, 31
Owego Times: 16
Owen, Alice: 3, 7, 10, 15, 17, 18, 26, 32, 33, 34, 38, 39, 40, 42, 45, 54

Pamunkey River, VA: 26, 27
Peninsula: 26
Pennsylvania Avenue, Washington, DC: 48
Perkins, Augustus S.: 5
Perkins, James H.: 24, 33, 37, 40
Perry's Victory (on Lake Erie): 48
Personius, Walker V.: 33
Petersburg, VA: 29, 30, 34, 47, 50, 55
Petersburg Road: 35
Pettes, William H.: 23

Picks: 2
Pierce, Cornelius M.: 24
Pillaging: 26
Ponton Train No. 4: 29, 30, 32, 33, 34, 35
Ponton trains: 6, 7, 8, 23, 25, 27, 28, 29, 30, 31, 33, 42, 46, 48, 50, 54, 55; canvas, 42; in park, 50; wagons, 55; *see also* Pontons, Ponton Train No. 4
Pontoniering: 23, 34
Pontoniers: 46
Pontons: 6, 26, 27, 28, 29, 33, 42, 46, 50; boats, 6, 26, 27, 30, 43; canvas, 30, 42; ferry, 6; wagons, 55; wooden, 26; *see also* Bridging Operations, Bridges, Ponton trains, Ponton Train No. 4
Pope, John: 2
Poplar Grove Church, Petersburg, VA: 41, 42, 43, 44, 45, 46, 47
Potomac River: 47
Powell, William H.: 48
Powhatan, Fort, VA: 29
Probasco, Theodore F.: 24
Putt: 1

Quartermaster duties: 29, 30, 31, 33, 34, 36, 41, 42, 46, 55

Raids: 27
Randall, James: 31
Rapidan River, VA: 14, 15, 25, 35
Rappahannock River, VA: 1, 5, 6, 15, 25, 52
Rappahannock Station, VA: 11, 12, 13, 14, 15, 16, 17, 18, 19, 20, 21 22, 23, 24
Recruits: 17, 18, 19, 39
Richmond, VA: 4, 26, 51, 52, 55
Roads: corduroy, 35; construction, 32, 47; repairs, 13, 47
Rogers, Randolph: 24
Rogers' bronze door: 24
Rosser, Thomas L.: 49

Salem Church, VA: 26
Scottsville, VA: 49
2d Corps: 25, 44
Sedgwick, John: 6
Seneca Falls, NY: 22
Seward, William H.: 53
Seymour, Horatio: 22
Shenandoah River, VA: 55
Sheridan, Philip H.: 26, 27, 37, 46, 55
Sherman, William T.: 55
Shovels: 2
Signal Corps: 44
Signal tower: 44, 47
Smyth, M. Truman: 55
Southside Railroad: 47
Spaulding, Ira: 6, 14, 23, 34
Spotsylvania Court House, VA: 25, 26, 27
Staunton, VA: 49
Staunton Pike: 49
Stephenson, VA: 55
Stevenson, Fort, Petersburg, VA: 40
Stockade: 23
Stoneman Station, VA: 4

Stratton, Charley R.: 31
Strawberry Plains, VA: 50
Surdam, Smith: 24
Susquehanna County, PA: 19

Tennessee: 11
3d Division, Cavalry Corps, Army of the Potomac: 29
Thomas Colyer, steamer: 46
Tools: 2, 47
Tower, signal: 44, 47
Trevilian Station, VA: 27
12th Corps: 11

Union, NY: 22
U.S. Sanitary Commission: 26
Uptons Hill, VA: 11

Van Brocklin, Martin: 29, 47
Vestal Broome, NY: 31
Virginia: 11, 26, 29
Virginia Central Railroad: 49
Volunteer Engineer Depot: 7, 23, 24, 48

Waldo, Lucius A.: 38
Warner, Mr.: 36
Warren, Gouverneur K.: 25
Warrenton Junction, VA: 11, 23
Washington, DC: 7, 8, 9, 10, 11, 19, 23, 24, 26, 46, 47, 48, 54, 55
Waynesborough (now Waynesboro), VA: 49
Weldon Railroad: 32, 34, 35, 36, 40, 43
White House, VA: 26, 27, 28, 29, 49, 50
Wilcox's Landing, VA: 28, 29
Wilderness Tavern (Old): 25
Williamsburg, VA: 2
Wilmington, NC: 45
Wilson, James Harrison: 29
Winchester, VA: 49, 55
Windmill Point, VA: 29
Woodbury, Camp, VA: 1

Yorktown, VA: 2, 19
Yorktown Battery No. 1: 19
Yorktown Battery No. 4: 19

Zoan Church, VA: 25, 26

☆U.S. GOVERNMENT PRINTING OFFICE : 1985—464-969/5-00078

www.ingramcontent.com/pod-product-compliance
Lightning Source LLC
Chambersburg PA
CBHW070813100426
42742CB00012B/2346